On Being Ninety

Jack Wicks

Wayne Umbreit

By
Jack Wicks
and
Wayne Umbreit

Copyright © 2003 by Jack Wicks &
Wayne Umbreit

ISBN0-7414-1589-5

Published by:

PUBLISHING.COM

519 West Lancaster Avenue
Haverford, PA 19041-1413
Info@buybooksontheweb.com
www.buybooksontheweb.com
Toll-free(877) BUY BOOK
Local Phone (610) 520-2500
Fax(610) 519-0261

Printed in the United States of America

Printed on Recycled Paper

Published July 2003

TABLE OF CONTENTS

Serious and Saucy Essays

Which Reminds Me

The Capitan Disc

Section 1

INTRODUCTION

We are writing of our thoughts and experiences when approaching the age of 90. That means that we were born about 1912 to 1913. So most of our childhood (to about 1925) was during the time of the First World War and the subsequent "early 20s" and we were undoubtedly affected by it. As young adults we made our way during the "Great Depression" when jobs were scarce and pay was low. We learned to survive on the minimum. In the mid-1920s we managed to get educated, and by 1935 began to get married, began to have children, began to make our careers, if not our fortunes. We faced the threat of the rise of the communist world. We lived through and participated in World War II. By 1975-80 we reached retirement, still able to get about. By the 1990s we could no longer physically manage the requirements of home maintenance and went into retirement homes--where we are now. Ours is called Twining Village and is in Holland, PA. It has about 400 residents, the great majority in the late 70's to mid-90's.

We have some experience in dealing with the aged, ourselves included, and after contact with the younger generation, we began to wonder if we might be of some use. Remember our children are in their 60's and are approaching retirement themselves and our grandchildren are in their 20s to 40s and are in the midst of their careers. But this younger generation has no idea what life is like at age 80 or 90, any more than we did at an earlier age. And not too many of us ancients are articulate enough to describe what life is like at these ages. It is quite possible that we are mistaken, but we think that we can describe such life and tell about interesting happenings in our lives that others might like to know. We do not want to preach nor to draw comparison with the 'good old days' now gone forever. But maybe you can catch the flavor of our lives by what we have to say now, and what we can remember of the past. And, if you are younger, this might amuse you and give you some preparation for the years to come.

We have too few pictorial illustrations of times gone by. Partly we can't remember where we put them if, indeed, we took them at all. Much of our early lives was photographed <u>via</u> the box camera, and, of course, in black and white. But then, in our opinion, we see too much imagery and too much rapid motion on television. So this presentation will be mostly devoted to the "18th century" essay—a useful art form that has almost disappeared. We hope you like it.

We have divided the presentation into four sections. One is the introduction which you are reading now. A second section contains essays of two or more pages. A third section is called "Which Reminds Me", giving brief descriptions of incidents in our lives which we remember. These are rather short; one page or maybe a little over. You will sometimes find a short piece in some other section. This is to save space. Brought up in the depression era we don't want to waste anything, even space. Of course this makes the book a little disorganized. But your life is not that tightly organized, so why should your books be? A fourth section is a little longer- a semi-science fiction novelette which you might enjoy on a quiet evening when you don't want to read too many possibly disjointed articles.

In all of this, we are not trying to give you a detailed outline of our lives, nor even a time-line of development, but only things that we remember and find interesting in our ninety years of living. We are told by the people who volunteer to keep the books in order in our library, that most people only read the books that are in large print, so we have put this in large print. But we also find that people our age have a little difficulty in attention span. We have therefore put together shorter pieces so that our attention can be more contained. We also find, that contrary to common belief among us, one does not have to read a book clear through. Although we still are products of our early youth and the depression; "the waste not –want not" idea. At any rate, this idea does not apply to reading, so skip about at bit and read what you like in any order, or in no order at all, as you might choose.

We find that listening to such adventures, or reading of them, triggers our own memory and brings back things long forgotten. We hope it will be your experience also.

Section 2
SERI0US AND SAUCY ESSAYS

A QUIET REVIEW OF AGING
(J. Wicks)

> "Sit here', you said,
> and pointed to the floor
> Where you sat playing with your
> toys
> and sit I did, of course,
> So we could more
> just play, like two young boys.
> How soon you left to romp
> with your new pup!
> I'm glad you didn't see
> how slow and painful getting up
> has now become for me.

Life keeps coming as a surprise to me, because I had no previous experience in being an old man. In recent days--well, all right, for several years, I have realized that I have acquired entirely too many possessions, and I suspect that you have also. Sometimes it seems that the possessions have acquired us, have taken over, and cluttered up the late portions of our lives. And nothing else can bring this situation to our attention quite as forcibly as the necessity to move from one residence to another, or, in the event of the death of someone close to us, the obligation to administer an estate. There must have been some reason for retaining every article, or some vague intention to do something with each possession, but the passage of time can erase the reasons and can blur the intentions.

When sheer necessity demands that we dispose of our own hoard of excess belongings, the difficulty is magnified when we learn that other people don't really want most of the treasures we are finally ready to give to them. The articles that can bring a warm glow of recollection and a welcome memory to us, can look to everyone else as trash. Our children and grandchildren, and here I speak with authority, even great grandchildren, are busy assembling for themselves their burden of excess possessions. Usually they don't need or want all the odd articles we have treasured during our lifetime. So, disposal becomes exactly that: disposing of things that we can't bestow on younger family members, even if we must unload everything on some local charity or discard it in trash dumpsters.

All this activity is painful enough, but it can become worse. Handling all the accumulated possessions of someone who has died can be difficult and confusing. It is challenging to try to determine what useful purpose somebody's long-kept treasures may ever have had, and to guess who might possibly want to inherit any part of a house full of goods which must be quickly removed. In disposing of our own accumulation, at least we know that we must have decided long ago that it was worth keeping. Understanding and handling another person's in-gathering of a lifetime can leave an administrator baffled and frustrated. What might some relative or friend or neighbor be delighted to acquire? Usually there is not enough time to seek out possible receivers. Unless antique furniture and Tiffany lamps and oriental rugs are involved, people are not standing in line to accept much. I know it can happen, because it has been my duty in recent years to fill plastic leaf-bags with countless articles belonging to now-deceased people who were dear to me, and to carry the bags to charity collection locations. Also, too many things that I considered had neither intrinsic nor sentimental value ended in trash dumpsters.

In a sense, clearing out the assembled collections of long over-kept possessions is saying farewell. It is good-bye not just to some material things, but also to years that have passed. We can pretend to ourselves that we are now mature enough to live today's life quite comfortably. Comfortably, that is, until discarding some reminders of almost forgotten years can leave us shaken and uncomfortable.

On an entirely different line of thought, there is another reminder. After almost half a century of frequent, practically constant, business travel, I can now be peacefully content without going any place. It is a complete change in lifestyle, and I find that I like it. Life now can be more like sitting on a rocking chair on the porch of a very old house located on a quiet side street of a small town. Forget New York and London and Bangkok and New Delhi and Singapore! They are in the past, and good riddance.

Then there is the subject of reading. Now, I recognize quality in style and in writing skill more than just concentrating, as I always did in the past, on quickly absorbing basic contents. Are writing skills so much better now than they have ever been, or am I finally learning how to read? A lifetime of quite intensive reading has developed into a deep appreciation of the best in classical and contemporary writing. What a long time it has taken!

Another new and somewhat surprising aspect of my advanced age is a realization that I really don't want anything more than, or different from, what I now have. What a difference! All through my younger years I wanted to obtain or to accomplish something more -something better. Perhaps that is what we call ambition. Or it may be more realistically defined as greed. Whatever it was, it was a strong motivator, an ever-present stimulus. Now in old age, I feel strangely contented with the present, without any urgent wish to improve or to replace anything.

Well, as I consider these random thoughts about aging, I think about one of my friends who is a retired psychiatrist, if retiring is possible. He probably says that all these symptoms reveal that I have experienced a mental fender-bender brought on by too many birthdays. The symptoms are quite clear. There is the difficulty of parting with the assortment of obsolete possessions accumulated over a lifetime. There is the peaceful accep-tance of the sudden ending of many years of travel. Another symptom is the radical change in reading habits. And don't forget the new-found contentment with almost everything and everybody. I can't deny the symptoms, so why should I resent this probably accurate diagno-sis?

For some reason I am reminded of the final line of "Gone With the Wind", "Frankly, my dear, I don't give a damn!"

ADVENTURES IN ETHIOPIA

(W. Umbreit)

When I was younger I belonged to an organization called GAAM which stood for "Global Aspects of Applied Microbiology". This organization, which had only a few hundred members, was nevertheless quite influential and was organized and directed by a group of excellent Swedish politicized scientists who shrewdly exploited the desire of third world politicians to make a mark for themselves in the world. Indeed, there was no good reason why microbiology, when applied to developing countries, could not have an important impact-- control of disease, improvement of crops, production of valuable materials (antibi- otics, solvents, etc.) from raw materials available in these countries that could be manipulated by microbiological methods. But from my point of view, it had one enormous advantage. It met, generally at the expense of the local government, in various parts of the world: Africa, India, Asia, the Mid East, South America, Mex- ico etc. At each of these countries we were given a royal welcome, given the best accommodations, and treated very well. I was the temporary head of the commission on education in microbiology and as such was invited to the directors meeting, met with the host institution and government officials, was given access to the universities and research institutes of the country being so "honored" by our visit—in short it was great even though, like many international organizations, it was something of a fraud. We had long discussions, drew up elaborate plans, but nothing ever really came of it. Still we had some nice trips and met some interesting people.

The trip I want to write about was taken in the fall of 1967 to Addis Ababa in Ethiopia. My wife and I flew to Athens, then spent a week exploring Greece. Incidentally, this was in late September, before the winter rains but after the tourist rush. The tour busses were not crowded, the tours are excellent—many being conducted by members of, or advanced students at, the major museums and universities. On the proper evening, at about 8 P.M., we flew from

Athens to Cairo (4 hours). These were propeller planes. At Cairo we were confined to the airport lounge for two hours, but at 2 A.M. we started our flight to Asmera in Ethiopia. The reason for this delay was that the Asmera airport had no lights so the planes had to wait till dawn before they could land there. This flight was about 3 hours. And we then flew down to Addis Ababa, the capital of Ethiopia. Here my wife and I were given a small cottage in the extensive "hotel" grounds. The hotel previously had been part of the palace of Haile Selassie, the "emperor" of Ethiopia. This cottage was quite nice except for two difficulties. The running water did not run except for a half hour between 2:30 and 3 in the morning. The story was that they were replacing the pipes and all would soon be fixed. It was not fixed during the week that we lived there. The main building of the hotel (the former palace) also had the same difficulty with water, but I think it is not hard to imagine (and I am certainly not going to describe it) the sanitary conditions which developed after the course of a week with perhaps 150 people living at the hotel.

The other difficulty with the cottage was that we had to cross a large enclosed square which had many trees. Now there was at that time, a visitor in one of the other cottages (presumably a fancier one than ours) who was some kind of an African potentate. I think, but I am not sure, that it was Idi Amin, but at any rate he traveled with about 20 bodyguards and there was one behind each tree (I think) in the square and until they got to know us, we had some difficulty getting to our cottage. They, of course, spoke no English and I never did find out what language they did speak, but we soon got on fine with them so that they no longer held sawed off shotguns (or maybe hand carried machine guns, after all, it was dark) at our heads when we returned to the cottage in the night.

The meetings took place in a brand new building, built at the emperor's orders for the OAU (Organization of African Unity). I got a good taste of African Unity when our organization decided to set up a training school, not in the developed countries like the U.S., England, France etc. but in some place not too far removed so that the students did not become too estranged from their native land and would return. I was given the task of organizing such a school. I never expected it to work and it didn't, but interestingly each African nation wanted the school on its own territory, which would defeat the original purpose entirely, but could have served a very useful purpose none-the-less. But not only did each want the school in his own country but was vehemently opposed to having the school in the country of his neighbor. We never got to the problems of what should be taught, who should teach it, or even who would finance it. So the major problems which would have to be faced were never even brought up. Since my diplomatic skills were not sufficient for this task, the project foundered. Looking back, it was perhaps an idea whose time had gone.

Ethiopia is a Christian country with a long history. Its rulers claim that the biblical Queen of Sheba was the ruler of Ethiopia and that they are therefore descended from Solomon and are equally wise. The church is Coptic Christian. We went to a service at the cathedral, and while I did not understand it, it seemed to me to be mostly chants with much waving of small 'Ethiopian' crosses. In the 1880-90s Ethiopia became a colony of Italy; in 1896 it gained its freedom from Italy, but in 1935 it was invaded by Italy, as part of the axis (Germany and Italy) push to conquer the world. Its young ruler (Haile Selassie) made a brilliant appeal to the League of Nations, which resulted in much respect for him and for Ethiopia, if not freedom from Italian rule. When the Italians were eventually expelled, Haile (born in 1892) was named regent in 1916, crowned emperor in 1930 and deposed by a communist revolution in 1974. He was killed by torture in 1975 [Incidentally, one can get lots of information on Ethiopia including his famous speech, from a Web search "Ethiopia"].

I had two distinct impressions of the "emperor" when I was there in 1967. One was that he rode about town in an old-fashioned fancy car which had a single raised back seat upon which he sat, enclosed in glass, for the admiration of the public. The impression was that of a tribal leader. Haile promoted the idea that he was for freedom of the individual and did indeed break up much of the feudal regional governments. It was alleged that any citizen could come see him and talk with him. One morning I had an appointment at the University and at an early hour, took a taxi which went past the rear of the palace. Here there was a long sidewalk leading to a gate which was filled with people waiting to see the emperor who would come to the gate at noon. Just before the gate, however, there were four large guards with long palm fronds which they beat over any person who came within their range. I was told that their purpose was to remove the flies from any person wishing to see the emperor, but they effectively discouraged any but the most physically enduring from entering. From his ancestry he called himself (maybe this was the title of his office) "The Lion of Judah". He kept a small zoo of lions on the Palace grounds (one could hear them roar at night) and two were stationed at the palace, one on either side of the gate. They looked a little mangy to me.

One evening Haile held a reception in the palace. We went, of course, and were introduced to him, and shook his hand. Without thinking, having nothing to say to such an eminent gentleman (if a little short of stature) I turned to leave and was seized by two burly guards and hustled off for turning my back on the emperor. The next morning, walking from the hotel to the meeting hall, I chanced to meet Martin Alexander, a soil microbiologist from Cornell. He inquired if I had been to the reception and had I noticed the Star of David. I recalled that I had, it was a part of the stained glass windows, it was woven into the rug, etc. As a joke, I said that of course since Haile was descended from the Queen of Sheba, and that was the house of David, you couldn't get anymore Jewish than that, to which Martin replied—"But he doesn't look Jewish".

Surprisingly, I had an ability to get along with and to understand strangers, no matter what language they speak, but in Ethiopia I found many English speaking people on the street, especially among the younger generation. I also saw an unusual phenomenon. At about 3 in the afternoon, just after school let out, there were numerous small crowds of children and young adults surrounding a "lecturer" both in the school yard and beyond. I learned that these were made up of people who did not have a chance at school (I don't know what the requirements were) but the idea was that if one learned something he should share it with those who did not have this chance at schooling. So that each day, those who had learned something at the school would tell those who had no chance to attend, what they had learned. English was a favorite subject for such discussion. As such, urchins, taxi drivers, porters, many tradesmen could speak a somewhat rudimentary English over and above their native variety of Amharic. This was very useful, since one could really talk to people and find out what they thought.

As a further example of this usefulness, it was suggested that if I went to the bazaar, I should hire the taxi driver, by the hour, to accompany me since he would be better able to bargain than I, and since I was paying him, he would be honest with me. I did this several times with surprising results. For example, I wanted to get a copy of the Book of St George, which is in the Coptic Bible but not in ours. I think that this is the same St George of St George of the Dragon of English tradition, but I am not exactly sure. My driver and I went to the bazaar. I explained what I wanted, but before he had translated it to the keeper of the stall advertising books, several young boys loitering around the place, dashed off in a hurry, returning with all sorts of religious objects—bands to put on the arm or forehead, etc.—generally saying "George". I knew and they knew that this was not what I was looking for, but what the heck, lets try it on this yokel. I did not find such a book in the Bazaar, and my driver really looked for it, but I did find a copy in a used bookstore in downtown Addis. It was leather bound, and smelled of camel-dung smoke, and was not excessively expensive—about $25 US as I remember.

I bought it and gave it to my son who was taking a course in comparative religions at his university, and among the faculty there was a man who could read Amharic. He was very excited about the book and said that it was one of the earlier renderings and that he wanted it to be donated to the University library. I really don't remember what happened to the book (and, of course, I couldn't read it) but this constituted for me a memorable adventure.

We were scheduled to fly to Beriut, stopping only at Khartum. This route took us over the origins of the Nile and straight up the Nile. We now knew something of the operations in Addis, so we left for the airport about 3 hours early. We were flying Mid-East Airlines. Throughout the mid-east area there are large billboards advertising Mid-East Air and I assumed that it was a large airline. Most such planes were operated by TWA pilots and were usually reliable. Today, however, on the air strip, there was a large Mid-East plane with one engine removed, the parts of which were lying on the ground. Natives were dashing about, picking up pieces and handing them to a mechanic on a step ladder to see if they would fit. While waiting, my wife got to talking with a lady who was also waiting, but more patiently than we, and it turned out that she was the wife of the Mid-East representative in Ethiopia. My wife suggested that since this plane did not look as if it was going to fly, why didn't Mid-east get another plane? The lady pointed out that they only had one other plane and it was in New Dehli. Eventually they got the plane together, tried it out and it flew—so we were off, some 5 hours late.

We went along the route of the Blue Nile till Khartumn, but there we found that the airport was under siege, because some revolution, quite common in those parts, having broken out. Without thinking I pulled out my camera to record this interesting scene, but was immediately surrounded by soldiers who were all for hauling me off to jail, if not shooting me right there. I managed to talk my way out

of this (probably by playing the fool tourist).

And we were soon on our way. The
pilot flew in an absolutely straight line up
the Nile to the Mediterranean, and we
could see below us the Aswan, Elephan-
tine, Abu Simbal , Karnak, the pyramids
etc. until he reached the Mediterranean,
went about 50 miles across the water
and then turned abruptly right into Beirut-
—civilization at last.

BORIS

(J. Wicks)

It seemed like any other day to me.
The trip to New York was comfortable
enough and Manhattan was having a
warm, sunny day in early May, 1985.
Instead of riding to the office I intended to
visit, I walked many city blocks, enjoying
the sudden change from cold winter
winds to soft, gentle breezes.There can
be something almost hypnotic about
those few perfect early Spring days.

The familiar office looked the same
as usual. How many times had I walked
in there in the twelve or more years we

had been friends, I wondered. All the people in the outer office greeted me. I put my hat in the coat closet as usual, and went into the office of the president of the company for the same happy, hearty exchange of greeting as always. We have been business friends and close personal friends for years. He accused me of having lost some weight-, I countered with the suspicion that he had gained some. Probably we were both right. Everything was normal, but there was no immediate mention of the business we were both impatient to complete. Instead, my friend said "Boris is here! You're just in time to celebrate with us, it's Boris' fortieth anniversary today."

He asked his secretary to bring Boris into the office and it took only a moment for tall, muscular—-and overweight—Boris, with his thick Serbian accent, his laughing, delighted greeting, his powerful handshake, to appear. I must have known him eight or ten of his sixty-eight or sixty-nine years, and he was always the same. He drank enough for two men, but he never showed any effects that I could observe. He ate more in one meal that I could eat in a whole day. If he ever felt tired, or bored, or discouraged, he never showed it. And I have been with him when he should, by all normal standards, have felt every one of those emotions. Boris, with a Yugoslav name that looks to English speaking people unpronounceable, with four consonants in a row before the first vowel?

Of course there was something different under the boisterous out-going surface. I knew that Boris and his wife had all their hopes and dreams wrapped up in their only son---a handsome intelligent giant of a youth busy collecting college degrees in the U.S.

Also I knew that Boris, in spite of holding an important position in the Yugoslavian government for over twenty years, had such an ill-concealed contempt for communism that he never got around to becoming a member of the Communist Party which ruled the nation he served. And then there was the matter of his retirement. Twice he was scheduled to retire at the mandatory age of sixty-five. Twice his records postponed the event, once by his birth date strangely becoming a year later than everybody knew right well, then by the records entirely vanishing into the mysterious void of lost files. The time did finally come, though, and Boris retired for a while to Belgrade. For weeks before he departed here were parties and farewell meals and bashes of every description. I was in New York for one of the affairs---a luncheon for eight at a favorite Yugoslav restaurant---a three hour meal with eight men enjoying the companionship and all pretending that there wasn't an undercurrent of sadness about nearing the end of Boris' years in the U. S.

In those years he had become an institution. He had devised and manipulated some impossible deals, involving importing and exporting, whatever Yugoslavia either needed urgently or wanted to dispose of quickly. Some of his explanations after completed transactions were hilarious classics of English with compound fractures of grammar and vocabulary.

So now it had come to pass that Boris and his wife were back in New York for several months to escape the dreariness of retirement in Belgrade. Even generous amounts of vodka and that deadly sweet and powerful plum brandy can not make Belgrade look like a city to anyone who has lived over twenty years in New York. It did not really matter what the three of us were going to celebrate; we would enjoy it because we are always comfortable together. More in courtesy than in curiosity, I suppose, I asked Boris what kind of an anniversary we were marking that day. When he told me, I was stunned. I said "Boris---I've known you all these years and you never mentioned this!"

His explanation was simple, expressed in his indescribable accent, and it was to the effect that he does not live in the past or in the future, because the present is "damn pretty good". We would celebrate that day, he told me, because "Forty year back from today I walk out of death camp." And then after a moment, the horror of a name, "Dachau".

ELEGANT SHOES

(W. Umbreit)

Which reminds me some months ago I awoke in the middle of the night because I could not breathe. I called our 'outpatient department' which sent for the ambulance. I had no time to dress and only managed to get on a pair of trousers and slip on some loafer type shoes. At the hospital (3 days) the technicians all remarked on what 'elegant' shoes I wore. They had rarely seen leather shoes. Evidently the canvas shoes are so common that one begins to notice leather shoes, however inelegant.

CZECHOSLOVAKIA

(W. Umbreit)

I spent some time in Czechoslovakia when it was under communist control. I found it rather austere and rather stiff, but these are some incidents I remember.

I and another American (whom I had not known previously, and whose name I can no longer remember) disrupted service in the main dining room of the Soviet-run hotel by introducing the nefarious act of tipping, not openly of course. We got service and what we wanted to eat, much to the consternation of a Russian group who could hardly get waited on. The hotel was a little outside of Prague and I normally took the street car to the older section. I looked somewhat like a German and if I would ask a question in English or in German, I would get no response. One day I made the trip with a Chinese fellow who asked exactly the same questions (sometimes prompted by me) and got copious answers. The latent hatred of the Germans was still present.

There was no love lost on the Russians either. I was waiting in the airport for a Soviet plane from Moscow to take me there. A Czech plane landed and was absolutely packed with people, both those coming from Moscow and those boarding to go to Moscow. After it left, my plane from Moscow arrived, one hour early. It was a large one, holding maybe 250 passengers. The doors opened and I was ushered aboard. The doors closed and we were off to Moscow 45 minutes before our scheduled departure time (How's that for promptness?) but except for me and three British business men who had been on the plane from good-ness knows where, the seats were empty. We made an effortless flight, and landed in Moscow where I was sent through customs rapidly into the main waiting room. I knew nobody, the people I was supposed to meet were delayed in Gander. I knew no Russian—what to do? I heard a man talking English with an American accent and he was holding a telegram and mentioned the word "Gan-der" in some puzzlement. So I ap-proached him and said that I was part of the 'antibiotic delegation' and was that what he was looking for? My luck was in, this was the welcoming committee (four of them) for the antibiotic delegation. The man himself, who spoke English, tried to pass himself off as an American visitor at the Ministry of Health, but if he didn't know what "Gander" meant, he had never done any international flying from the States as he claimed. But why should

I tell him? In my opinion most undercover operatives are exposed by such little accidents that no one could predict. At least he took me to the hotel where I had reservations (made by the ministry of Health of the USSR). This was the Ukraina. The clerk at the desk took one look at me and assigned me to the Chinese section—so all the instructions were in either Russian or Chinese, both of which I know equally well, namely not at all. So this was my introduction to the Soviet Union.

Which also reminds me that I had an unusual insight into the feelings of the people toward the USSR. I was attending an antibiotic conference in Prague, but I got in late and the members had all gone to the little town of Melnick for dinner so I was sent there, together with an East German who had also just arrived. They spoke no English but asked if I spoke German (I don't remember how they asked me). I told them that I did not. I forgot to tell them that I could understand it fairly well, especially if it were "low" German. So we started out, the East German asking the driver how things were in Czechoslovakia and getting a reply that things were terrible, to which he agreed that they were no better in East Germany. From there on I heard a litany of what was wrong with both governments. It is better that I do not remember it. Incidentally Melnick is famous for its wine, and over the door of the magnificent church there is the statement "In Vino Veritas"= In wine there is truth.

I attended a banquet in the magnificent town hall. The waiters prided themselves on knowing English, but all they could say was "I like Ike". In the course of the evening, I needed to find the rest rooms. After some discussion with the waiter, using the necessary gestures, I was directed down the hall to another large room. It was made entirely of mirrors and extended at least 100 feet, being punctuated on both sides by doors about every 20 feet. They were all labeled in Czech. Which was the one I wanted? Since the need was urgent, I opened one labeled, so far as I could tell, with a gothic "P". And, of all things, it was the right one! One proceeds happily through life (to be profound) if one's luck is good.

The Soviet-run hotel where I stayed in Prague had magnificent "Turkish" coffee. And I drank quite a bit of it. The net result was that I could not sleep nights (until I discovered the cause). But while awake I would look out over a rather large medieval square. And frequently, the army (Czech or Soviet?) would use the square to practice street fighting.

One day walking with a Czech friend we passed a fast food restaurant (this was before McDonalds took over). I remarked that this curious western custom was becoming established in Europe. He drew himself up, insulted, and said that the restaurant had been here, serving food the same way, for over 300 years.

When I went to Prague, relations with the USSR were reasonably friendly. But there was a turn for the worse and Khrushchev claimed that he was going to take over Berlin unless the US apologized more fully for sending spy planes over the USSR. I did not think he would do it, but I did not wish to be behind the 'iron curtain' in case it should happen. This was a Tuesday. I thought to go to Vienna and come back on Sunday because I had reservations on the Moscow flight from Prague and permission to enter the USSR on that flight (only). However, there was a complication. I had come in by air and the rules said I must leave by air, but I could book no flights out of Prague—they were all full. Besides I wanted to leave by train, there was the famous 'spy' train, the 'Mid-Europa Express" which starting in East Berlin went through East Germany, through Dresden, then Prague, then came out to western controlled Austria, then went back again through Hungary and finally to Istanbul. I took my problem to the Czech passport office where a very kindly older lady said that she would see what she could do, but I had to leave my passport with her. I had scheduled a two day tour to the High Tatras, a resort area on the Polish border but I would be back by Friday on which day she thought she could get permission for me to leave by train.

So I traveled in the High Tatras without a passport, but with a group of tourists conducted by the Czech tourist agency. On coming into a hotel, of course, we had to check in, and they always wanted my passport. I explained that the police had it in Prague but its number was 'USA xxxx' any number that came into my head. This was perfectly satisfactory, all they wanted was something to fill in the space on a form. The High Tatras were a tourist resort with many fine hotels built by the British. They were now used for the occasional groups of tourists, such as mine, but mostly as 'rewards' for workers in the USSR who had produced beyond their quota. These people were not very happy. The luxury of the British hotel (somewhat austere by our standards) was unfamiliar to them. Many slept in the halls, rather than disturb the bedroom (Maybe they regarded them as museum displays). This group was led by a Czech guide, a very charming young lady who spoke Czeck, Russian and French. The only words of English she knew (or so she said) were "I love you". It was difficult to keep up a reasonable conversation even if she was a wonderful dance partner. She eventually was cornered by a charming Italian who spoke French—how well I do not know.

I returned to Prague early Friday morning and my passport and exit permit were available. I picked up the train about 10 A.M. and was met by an agent of the tourist bureau who refunded some money because we had not gone to a place scheduled on the tour. Real basic honesty, until about 20 minutes out of Prague, we were stopped at a border checkpoint and all the money was confiscated since it could not be exported. On that train there was a charming white haired old lady who was exceedingly nervous. She passed the border checkpoint without trouble and began to brighten up. We were traveling down the Danube valley and it was really beautiful.She said "When I was a child, this was all one country. We can hope that it will be again".

DAMASCUS — IMPRESSIONS

(J. Wicks)

Syria is a country governed by a war-oriented dictatorship. It is ready for hostilities. As the plane circled the Damascus airport, I was impressed by the size of the military installation adjoining the airport. As the plane landed, I was uncomfortable to see the anti-aircraft gun emplacements bristling close to the landing strips. Syria obviously has no intention of allowing any plane to land there without permission. I had no visa. Syria does not even maintain a consular representative in New York, and if there had been one, I doubt that I would have qualified for a visa. The airport was not air-conditioned. It was hot. A brilliant sun dazzled my eyes. Almost all the people I saw were Arabs, dressed in the long, loose robes they prefer, with men wearing the draped cloth headdress typical of desert countries. Women just arrange their shapeless ankle-length robes to cover their heads and to conceal their feet. It was not a promising start for a visit to historic, mysterious Damascus.

Also, there were some official forms to be filled in, and some discussions with airport authorities about whether I must remain in the transit area of the airport for many hours, or do as I requested, which was to see the city. They agreed, not because of any bribes, but because it looked as if I might spend all my available hours arguing with them if they did not agree to let me leave the stifling transit area and visit the city. Bureaucracy is about the same wherever you encounter it. Syria is a Middle Eastern country which has produced warriors, craftsmen, religious leaders, and above all else, outstanding business men and women. Syrian accountants and bookkeepers are respected in every country where business is important. This is a country apparently without the extraordinary natural advantages of many of its Arab neighbors in the form of huge petroleum deposits. It is a land of sun-scorched mountains and valleys, and vast rocky areas. It is a place where any oasis of green growth is beautiful, and appreciated. Here, people have had to work hard, or think intensively (or both) for survival. These are people I can understand and appreciate - and I found them quick to accept me as an interested observer -not as an American sightseer who should be relieved of his money in every way possible. I approached Syria, and especially Damascus, with respect and interest and a feeling of walking on ground that was somehow important in the history of mankind. I entered Damascus with the attitude of one lonely American who had probably encountered a total of only 5 or 6 Syrians in a lifetime and who had respected and admired each one of them.

There were several ancient taxis outside the airport; none of the drivers spoke English. But an Army policeman did, and he told one of the drivers in Syrian a long and detailed plan which I hoped included my simple wishes. The road to Damascus seems to have been carved out of the flat stone which is much more common than soil in that area. The taxi traveled at moderate speed, but the bone-jarring shocks convinced me that the body was part of the frame of the car, with no springs between. The first traffic we encountered, after a mile or more, was a man leading a camel which was heavily loaded with some kind of freight. Then we saw men leading -and some riding - donkeys. The thought kept coming to my mind that much of what I was seeing, after I had passed by the military installation, was quite likely almost unchanged from Bible times. Houses were made of earth and wood. Fences were built of layers of earth, baked by the intense heat of the sun, and protected by a layer of straw on top which I suppose guards against the fence turning to mud in a rain storm.

Part of Damascus is in a valley, and much of the city is built on a steep hillside. The city's streets are winding, and any one street is alternately wide and narrow, which is an effective way of enforcing speed limits. Every narrow section is a bottleneck through which traffic moves slowly and noisily.

No conversation was possible between the driver and me. But when I saw a sight which pleased me, I said "Oh!", and pointed to it. He grinned and offered me a cigarette. I shook my head that I did not smoke, but I offered him a package of American chewing gum, which he accepted. Then he gave me a piece of my chewing gum. It required a long time to see Damascus from the hilltop and to thread our way into the busiest part of the city. The driver's thumb was on the horn almost steadily - not to warn other cars, for they were few, but to urge pedestrians to save their lives by moving out of the taxi's way at the last possible moment. I am sure I was much more tense and worried than the pedestrians were.

We stopped at an entrance to a building which led to another entrance back in the darkness. The driver called to an elderly Syrian who hurried over to open the door of the taxi for me. He spoke a very little English, and tried to assure me that my driver would wait while I visited the Mosque of Omayad. Since I had not paid the taxi driver, I felt pretty sure he would wait, no matter what I wanted to do. Besides, the Syrian did speak some very broken English, which is much better than none at all.

It developed that he was a guide, specializing in the mosque. I formed the impression that he would have happened to specialize in anything I wanted to see in Damascus. He was sturdy, weathered to a leather-like color, and he smiled easily. In the first minute or two, he groped for an English word and substituted its French equivalent. I asked in French if he spoke that language. That released a torrent of French, seasoned with some English; we had established excellent communications.

"Did he speak French, one asks! Had he not personally escorted Monsieur Pompidou before he become President of France, through the very mosque we were about to enter? Like his own mother tongue, he spoke French!" He was well-informed, interesting, and very likeable. We removed our shoes and entered through the dark entrance to the most startlingly beautiful building I had ever seen. The Mosque of Omayad has been a Roman temple, a Byzantine church, an Orthodox church, and is now a Moslem mosque. The huge expanse of floor is completely covered by Oriental rugs and carpets laid side by side. Two thousand of them, according to my guide. The ceiling is decorated with the most ornate designs in many colors and with intricate outlines in gold. Colored glass windows are almost beyond belief in complexity and sheer radiance.

Many men, and a few women, sat on the floor at worship or contemplation. There are no seats or benches. Men at prayer were on their knees, with their foreheads touching the floor. It was silent. No one paid any attention to me, although I was obviously a foreigner in their midst. It was deeply impressive. Close to the very center of the mosque is a building within the building, about twenty feet long and ten or twelve feet wide, and probably twenty feet high. It is a treasured Christian relic inside a Moslem mosque -the tomb of Saint John the Baptist. My guide showed me the vast enclosed courtyard, the minaret, the collection of manuscripts and hand-lettered books, and spoke quietly and interestingly about everything. He was as patient and considerate as any man could be. Our governments might have serious differences, but he and I appreci-ated the same things and spoke the same language and instinctively liked each other.

As I started to pay his fee for about a half hour of intelligent assistance, he asked if I would like to visit a shop in the arcade of stores adjoining the mosque. Of course I would. We entered a shop which seemed only about as large as a passenger elevator in the U.S. The owner produced merchandise from shelves, boxes, the floor, even from cords hanging from the ceiling. He asked quite high prices. After buying a supply of postcards, I moved to the door, to leave, with a quiet comment that the prices were too high for me. Then began a three-way price-haggling session in Syrian, French and English, which we all enjoyed immensely. Another tourist came to the entrance of the shop, and seeing the obviously heated argument among the shopkeeper, the guide and me, departed to a quieter, safer shop across the street.

When we reached a grudging compromise on the price of the few articles I wanted to take home, I paid the shopkeeper and the guide and was ready to return to the taxi. That, it developed, was out of the question. "Would I prefer Turkish coffee, or tea, or soda?" Turkish coffee is a mixture of powdered coffee and cocoa, boiled to a thick, black consistency more like syrup than coffee. I would have liked that, but I asked for some of "that fine Syrian tea'. They both beamed with pleasure. We were three men who had never seen each other before, and almost certainly would never encounter each other again. For a few moments over tiny glasses of tea we all enjoyed each other's company. Outside the shop, the sun was bright and hot. The taxi moved slowly because of the throngs of people who paid almost no attention to the shrill horn. Everywhere there were uniformed soldiers, off—duty. Tiny donkeys trudged along the streets, loaded with many kinds of burdens.

I was happy to be in Damascus.

POEM

(J. Wicks)

> My uncouth ways of by-gone days
> Were rightly blamed on youth.
> Now that I'm old it must be told
> I'm neither kempt nor couth.

INCIDENTS IN IRAN

(W. Umbreit)

I first went to Iran, (Teheran, of course) via the night plane from Istanbul. Seated next to me was a very pleasant fellow who was, it turned out, the minister of education. He spoke excellent English, and we happened to both know members of a prominent Iranian family, the Farmafarmanians—so we discussed a variety of topics and he gave me some very useful hints as to what to see in the country. It came time to serve cocktails, so I pointed out that I had the advantage in that I could drink them and that he was restricted by his religion to soda. He said, that I did not understand, that the prophet was all knowing, and had stated in the

47

Koran, that if one was in a country or a situation where one wished to remain unnoticed, that one could conform to the customs of the country, without violating the teachings of Allah, but it just happened that he did not like alcohol so he was content.

We arrived about 1 AM and after a very rapid custom check, I got a cab to my hotel. The cab stopped before a rather shabby building, the entrance to which was lighted by two flaming oil torches. Well, after all this was oil country so why not? What surprised me later was to see dealers in pushcarts selling kerosene by the quart or gallon (some in milk bottles) to the housewives for use in lamps. The hotel clerk spoke a good American and I was soon in my room, but never having been here before, I was rather worried about what might be in store for me. I knew no one. In the morning I went down for breakfast, to find the entire dining room speaking in American and aside from the waiters, there were few Iranians. It turned out that this hotel was the favorite of the foreign workers, mostly American, who worked in the oil fields of the Gulf. Not surprisingly it had an excellent bar. After breakfast, I got a cab to take me to see the "Crown Jewels". While they were excellent, even better was the idea behind this display. So far as I can tell, Crown Jewels do not draw interest and are expensive to keep since they must be carefully guarded. But here were a set of government assets that were being shown to the public (for a fee, of course) and could thus serve as a source of revenue. At the same time they could be used by the government as collateral for borrowing.

I returned about noon, to find the bar full of the people I had breakfasted with. I forget how I spent the afternoon (I think it was a tour of the Shah's palace), but when I returned for supper, the same people, now joined by others, were having a riotous time in the bar. They insisted that I have a drink. So, remembering Allah, I did. I then tried to get reservations to Isfahan and Shiraz. The planes were all full and I was 29th on the waiting list. The fellows at the bar assured me that there would be plenty of room on the plane (which proved to be

the case) because they all held reservations on it, but had no intention of going
back to work until their leave was over by
several days. They said that this extra
absence was a good thing as it caused
the Iranians to become more independent. So, in spite of being 29th I got to
Isfahan.

I was most impressed by the large
rectangle (called the 'Maridan") and with
the buildings surrounding it. I had a guide
who took me through the various notable
buildings but I was most impressed when
he led me into the "Blue Mosque" and
said sincerely (not just a tourist gimmick)
"You know I have come to this place
every Friday for my entire life. And I am
still impressed by its quiet beauty and by
all the memories it stirs in me when I
kneel to pray." I stayed at a rather nondescript hotel and after an excellent meal
one evening I stopped at the desk to
inquire as to whether it was safe to go
out alone. There were no street lights
and the bazaar, where I wished to go in
search of some coins of the medieval
period (in which my son was interested),
the bazaar was lighted only with lamps or

smoky fires on little stone "alters" and almost everyone wore a dagger. When I inquired as to the safety, the desk clerk was astonished. Why did I ask? Well, I said, it would not be safe to go on the streets in New York without some protection. He said "What kind of a place must New York be, when you cannot go safely to bazaar at night?" Incidentally I did find the coin I was looking for and bargained, over a cup of tea, with a bearded, I would call him Bedouin, in a mixture of languages—and found him to have much more knowledge about such coins than I. When I returned home experts here said that I had paid a modest price for it.

Isfahan boasts one of the best hotels in the world, the Shah Abbis, and when later I took my wife to Isfahan, that is where we stayed. It lived up to its reputation. We were there shortly before Christmas and the lobby was decorated with Christmas trees, this in a Muslim country. When I was there first, I happened to stop into a shop showing miniature paintings and got to talking with the artist who made them. The apprentices painted the borders but the pictures of the famous buildings were painted by him. He invited me to sit beside him while he painted, in very delicate strokes, a scene from the center of ancient Isfahan. I purchased one, about 5 inches wide and four inches high which I have to this day. Some four or five years later, when I took my wife, we happened upon his shop and stopped in. Of all things, he remembered me, possibly I was the only customer who ever bought anything. The bazaar in Isfahan is not necessarily a tourist attraction, but is actually the place where they manufacture many things, some cheap and gaudy, but some delicate in nature. I remember seeing a man shape a metal tray using a hammer and an electric drill.

I next went to Shiraz and met a German scholar who was stationed there and to whom I was introduced through some friends of mine in the States. He took me on a party given by the Shah in a 'Persian Garden' with dancing girls and all the trimmings, this just 8 hours flying time from New York (It took me longer) but a world away. I went down to Persepolis, the palace of the Persian Kings, and saw Darius's palace. I had wanted to go on to the tomb of Cyrus, but never got there. I particularly wanted to see the tomb of Cyrus because of its inscription which I understand reads *"Ah stranger, from wherever thou commest, and come I know thou wilt, I am Cyrus, King of the Persians. Envy me not this paltry earth that covers my bones."*

Three things impressed me in Shiraz. One was the tomb of Saadi, regarded in Iran as the preeminent poet of Persia. Ohmar Kyam is regarded as a minor poet of no special significance. I had never heard of Saadi and what I have read of him seems crude. He lacks a translator of the genius of Fitzgerald to make his poems come to life for a westerner. Another impression was that there was a certain amount of electric street lighting (not all lights worked) and underneath each pole on which the light was working would be clustered a group of students studying because the light was much better here than in their homes. On the day I was to leave the German scholar said "I will pick you up at 5 AM to show you something", which he did although my flight was not till 10 AM He took me to a mosque whose courtyard was full of young men walking up and down and sometimes in circles, muttering something. There must have been about 150 of them. He said that they were learning the Koran and they had to know a requisite number of verses by heart before they could go on to higher education. I said that this seems to be an inordinate number of students and he said, well these were the ones who had failed the exam and were studying with a hope they could pass the next one.

Two other incidents remain in my memory. My wife was afraid of cats and one time when we checked into the Iran Hilton (right below the mountain range) we had a cocktail in the lobby cocktail lounge and there was a large cat crawling among the potted trees that were part of the décor. This upset my wife, so I went to the desk to see if someone would remove the cat. The bell boy, took a look at the cat and said, "Lady, I would give my life for you, but I am not sure that I can handle that cat". Another time we were given rooms on the 14th floor of a downtown Tehran hotel. The wall air conditioner had been removed from the wall of the hotel and no attempt had been made to cover its space so we had an open space in the wall fourteen stories up.

POETIC MUSE

(J. Wicks)

Who really grasps and understands my deep poetic muse? Youse!
Who is the one whose thoughts create soul-satisfying rhyme? I'm!
Who will develop limpid grace in new unprecedented style? I'll!
Will connoisseurs appreciate each new poetic step? Yep!
Will I be published? Can I even hope?
Nope!

DEVELOPMENT OF PUBLIC HATRED

(J. Wicks)

Observing the successful creation and spreading of massive hatred is an alarming and discouraging spectacle, but it is also a study of applied psychology in action. There may never be an end to the explanations and recriminations pertaining to the Hitler years in Germany. A much more recent example, and one less documented for public consumption was, and still is, Iran.

How did an ally of the U.S., the beneficiary of tremendous financial and military and political generosity become enraged and contemptuous of every aspect of America? There are always volumes of official explanations of major developments, especially those that turn out badly. Written in obscure political and diplomatic styles, they are embalmed in incomprehensible bureaucratic language. They are not intended for public information and would be useless if they were widely distributed.

That type of official recording would dwell at length on the decaying condition of the government of Iran for many years before the outbreak of violent anger against the U.S. And that much would be entirely accurate. Many years of the rule of the Shah Mohammed Rezi Pahlavi were an interval of almost unbelievable corruption. The government oppressed the masses while lavishly providing luxuries to the family, relatives, friends and co-conspirators of the royal family. Rich Iranians took advantage of the poor. Educated Iranians abused the ignorant. Privileges were sold to the highest bidders. And yet, for years there was no overt effort toward rebellion or correction.

Almost incredibly, all the countries which profitably dealt commercially and militarily with the Shah's Iran quietly accepted the prevailing conditions. And foremost among these countries was the U.S. It probably would be an exaggeration to record that one man organized, developed, and conducted the program which caused the complete reversal of a nation the size of Iran. But it would be very close to the truth.

An elderly Moslem fanatic named Ayatollah Khomeini lived in Paris after being expelled from Iran because his ostensibly religious activities showed symptoms of developing from a nuisance into successful rabble-rousing. He possessed a remarkable asset which ultimately converted his status from chronic annoyance into world power; he knew how to use the tremendous potential available in creating and disseminating and infecting a nation with a combination of religious fervor and raw hatred. Making use of the religious nature of Iranian Shiite Moslems, he prepared highly inflammatory sermons for mullahs to deliver to Friday throngs in mosques throughout the cities and towns in Iran. From the very beginning he emphasized three targets for the venom of religious hatred: (1) The Shah and all his family and retinue; (2) all Jews; and (3) the United States.

Attacking the Shah was no real novelty. Small troublesome groups had done that for years with no noticeable results. Law enforcement was so lax that there was usually no excitement or publicity even when occasional agitators simply disappeared. However, vicious evidence against the royal family became much more effective when presented by mullahs in the religious atmosphere of weekly services in mosques throughout the nation.

Attacking Jews was a fairly easy way to generate hatred. In the strange economy of Iran, two major business activities were successfully, and profitably, dominated by Iranian Jews. The two activities were banking and retailing. The Ayatollah touched a sensitive nerve when he directed rage and hatred against Jewish control of the financial network of banking and the commerce of retailing. The effectiveness of the anti—Jewish program became visible in even minor everyday contacts with Iranians. The last few times that I had work to do in Iran, I could see a change taking place. A Tehran citizen, whom I knew well, asked me who represented me when I was away from the country. When I told him, he asked whether I realized that it was a Jewish firm. He suggested that I change representatives at once. When I declined to change, our friendly relationship chilled. Even a good taxi driver whom I liked to charter by the full day every time I went to Tehran spoke openly. After he waited for me to conduct some dealings with an old Tehran establishment, I returned to the taxi. He asked me whether I knew that I had been dealing with a Jew.

This aging religious radical in Paris was spreading hatred thousands of miles away. And he shrewdly associated the growing hatred of Jews with a parallel contempt for the U.S. The long-standing American support of Israel became a powerful weapon against everything which the U.S. had loaned, sold, or given to Iran during the reign of the tottering Shah. By the time that the Ayatollah triumphantly returned to Iran, his personal radiation of obsessive intense hatred had deposed the Shah, had driven out of the country most of the Jews who could afford to leave, and had changed the whole nation from successful co-operation with the U.S. to bitter, destructive enmity. It would always be a serious mistake to underestimate the sheer power of hatred.

EPICURE via COMPUTER

(W. Umbreit)

As a person who came to use a computer somewhat late in life, I am continually amazed at how it surprises me. Of course, I don't understand how it works, but then I never did understand how a television could work or even a radio, yet I am able to use them quite successfully. But the computer is different. Every once in a while it does some surprising things. For example, my grandson called me and wanted to know the meaning of "epicure". Now he has been brought up with computers, but seems to regard them as a source of games and music and chat rooms, but rarely does he seem to try to derive information. After talking with him I decided to look at the net and see what information was there that he was missing so I could admonish him not to disturb my afternoon nap. I started with a simple definition (which I got from the dictionary, i.e. an epicure is "a person who has a refined taste in eating and drinking"). There were 69 "matches". I usually look at the first ten and if these don't fit with what I want, I try some other word. These ten touted some vegetarian restaurants, a coffee magazine. a store selling chocolates, and a few restaurants. I then tried "epicurious" (I must have misspelled something) but I got 183 items which were mostly recipes for Indonesian, or Jewish, or Mediterranean foods. etc. I then tried "Epicurean" which my dictionary said was "a person devoted to pleasure and luxury". Here I got 187 matching sites which were mostly set up by "epicurean" societies and people offering to cook epicurean meals in your own home. I left the computer for a while and when I returned I called up "epicurian" (misspelling 'epicurean'). Here I hit a jackpot of information (294 matches) most of which I did not previously know. See how the computer can broaden your mind! First there was a 'burstnet.com' which I gather offered swim suits. Then there were four hits called "swimsuit gallery" (all identical). So I looked at one of these. It gave me a home page containing 25 "thumbnail" photographs of young ladies in various swimsuits enlargable and in full color! One could click onto other very similar pages labeled 'attractive' or 'divine' or "epicurian" or "suggestive" etc , some 20 of them. So altogether there were 20 times 25= 500 presumably different types of swimsuits. I don't know this for sure because I did not check out all of these pages to make sure that a given swimsuit did not appear on more than one; that is, a swimsuit could be 'attractive" and "suggestive' and thus could appear on two such pages. But at least there were a lot of swimsuits. One did not need to buy the swimsuit edition of "Sports Illustrated" or something like that. I wondered how many types of male swimsuits there were but I could not find any information. I would guess that there are not more then ten. Clearly the female has an enormously better choice.

Also among the first ten matches there was something called "glamour gallery". There were four of these, which seemed to be identical. Clicking on to one of these I got a page similar to that of swimsuits but with attractive young ladies in different types of lingerie. There were some 500 of these as well. How the people at "Playboy" must cringe. I had no idea that there were so many types of lingerie. Again men's choices are much more limited, especially if you do not count as a special type, the shorts given me for Christmas which were imprinted with yellow butterflies. I did not have a chance to examine these things further, since at that point the electricity went off for five hours. I do not think that I did it and I do not know if it is proper for me to return since I now know what this item contains and have clearly been given a signal to desist. But think for the moment about how much possibly useful information I accumulated. Clearly one needs correct spelling (a notorious deficiency in the young) since the computer responds to what seem to be simple requests. How one can "protect" the young from such information? Even the term lingerie creates a problem. How do you pronounce it (let alone spell it?)? The word itself evidently came from the Greek "linon" meaning flax and from this same root we get the words, linen, lint, linseed and even linoleum. Men do not have lingerie, only underwear. And just think of the choices and decisions a female has to make in deciding what to wear, whereas we males pick up whatever is in the drawer without much further thought except, is it big enough? Of course, women do not need to pick out one of the five hundred every day-they can pick among those which they have pur- chased- presumably a somewhat smaller choice. I heard a television commentator bemoaning the choice that women make in choosing "cheap" lingerie. He said "One may purchase a $2000 gown but spoil it by purchasing cheap ("$200") underthings". Clearly men have the great advantage, they can buy shorts pack- aged by the dozen at a comparatively low price and do not need to mortgage the farm just to get to wear something that nobody sees anyway. As I said, the computer is full of surprises, which is a better recommendation than to say that it is educational.

GREEK ENCOUNTER

(J. Wicks)

It seems fair enough to use a Greek word,-'chaos'- to describe evening traffic around Independence Square in Athens. Most of the cars and taxis are small in size; their maneuverability and speed and the noise of their horns are astonishing. And yet, looking down on the scene from the glass enclosed roof-top dining room of the King George Hotel in early dusk made it seem somewhat less frantic, less chaotic.

We were three elderly men, seated at one of the preferred tables beside the front window where we could see the busy Square and the buildings facing it, with all those advertising signs spelled out, of course, in Greek letters.

Our host for the evening was Basil; he and I had been friends, both business and personal, for eight or ten years. His other guest, Nikos, had been a friend of Basil's since they were a pair of young hellions many years before. They were expensively dressed in very good taste. Basil was an official in a shipping company that at that time owned the largest fleet of Greek-registered ships in the world. Nikos owned a small company that had only a few dry-cargo ships, all of which were extremely profitable.

Ordering dinner was a slow and serious matter, as indeed it should be. We considered the recommendations of the maitre d' and decided against his ideas about wine selection and accepted his suggestions about the main course of dinner.

Then we talked. And ate, of course, but mostly I remember that we talked, quietly and easily, enjoying each others' company. We savored the French wine which they insisted would be better than my choice of a modest Greek wine, and probably was much better.

Basil told Nikos, with some embellishment, about my arrival in Athens that same day from London, overloaded with luggage for a long trip to Egypt and I forget where else, also carrying all the scotch whisky I could handle, as a gift for Basil. It wasn't just any scotch, but a particular favorite of his, an obscure brand, which because of scarcity or perhaps sheer indolence, has never been exported outside the United Kingdom. In turn, that led to an involved story about one of Nikos' chartered freighters which even then lay anchored offshore from a Nigerian port, collecting an outrageous amount of demurrage while waiting its turn to unload in the hopelessly crowded port. The captain of the ship had been rather enjoying the complete inactivity until a recent grim day when the ship's stores of scotch and every other form of alcohol were finally exhausted. Only then did the dried-out captain start using all his Greek wiles to locate someone who could be bribed or blackmailed into arranging for emergency unloading of his cargo. Actually the cargo bore no faint resemblance of emergency importance to Nigeria. The ship was heavily loaded with cement. The meal was leisurely and excellent.

Then a group of men came in for a dinner party and were seated not far from our table. There were five Greeks and one European who proved to be a Frenchman. The Greeks were all shipping men who were acquainted probably as competitors rather than as friends, I thought, with Basil and Nikos. They exchanged greetings from a distance and sat down with their guest. At first they really did try to keep their conversation in French, but that didn't last long. Soon there were torrents of Greek all around and across the table. A couple of times the Frenchman and I exchanged glances and he gave what I thought was a rueful smile. All his companions were heavy, sturdy middle-aged men who showed visible effects of living the good life. I doubt that there was one of them who weighed less than 200 pounds. The Frenchman, on the other hand, was quite the opposite. He was at least as old as the others, and he appeared to me to be years older than any of them. He was thin and straight and wiry. He looked almost dwarfed, surrounded by his heavyweight friends. When he and I talked briefly, later in the evening, his thin face and slim form made the contrast with his companions even more acute. In that setting, at that moment, the man appeared almost frail.

As I write this, my thoughts keep

returning to that rather quiet slender Frenchman and the look of frailty among his beefy friends. But you can't judge by appearances. For years he worked harder than most men half his age, directing and performing rigorous research far beneath the surface of the oceans of this world.

He was Jacques Cousteau.

LONDON LUNCH
(J. Wicks)

It is very easy to love London. In spite of its often uncomfortable weather. the city has always had a way of casting a spell on its natives and on visitors. Every other major city that I have seen is really a composite of nationalities and cultures and foibles, but London alone was what it has always been, the very essence of all that is British, for good or for bad, with apologies to nobody. I have had friends who return to London as regularly as their occupations and their finances make possible, from the far reaches of the world, and I have done the same thing in the years past.

Not that everything is perfect, of course. As fascinated as I have been with riding through miles of cluttered London streets, and as happy as I have been when trudging through many sections of the city right up to the point of physical exhaustion, there are some features of the place that do not appeal to me at all. And one of those features is English restaurant meals. There are some outstandingly fine restaurants in London, but the best of them, for my taste, are French or some other specialized dining rooms. In my own observation, typical English restaurant meals in London are usually mediocre. And that includes some beautiful and very expensive establishments.

But the time I am thinking about now was different. I had a business conference appointment with a good friend, in his office. His London headquarters was in an ancient building in Bishops gate, that area of weathered commercial structures that look as if they must date back a hundred and fifty years or more. The street is named Saint Helen's Court. It is short and narrow, a relic of long forgotten days.

My friend's Bentley was parked in the only parking space near the entrance of the building. His firm occupied many floors of the structure. As chairman of the board and owner of the majority of shares in his group of companies, he had a suite of offices that could have accommodated an entire medium-sized company. The lift, entered from the lobby, which was a venerable cage of ornamental iron work, operated by an aged Londoner who watched closely as the car rose floor by floor, almost as if he wondered whether the strain might be too much for the whole apparatus.

Every detail of the building was very old and thoroughly English. Lighting in the hallways was just barely adequate. Lighting fixtures were ornamental but inefficient. The woodwork all through the building was oak, darkened by who knows how many coats of varnish and by generations of air pollution.

The position of private secretary to the chairman is no trivial assignment. She was short and sturdy, with a beautiful English complexion. She was dressed in no—nonsense tweed skirt and jacket. We had often talked, she and I, in trans-Atlantic telephone calls, and in my visits to her boss, but I never had even a vague idea of her age and I still have none. She could have stepped right out of one of those excellent British television plays -- so dignified, courteous and very reserved. She took me this time to the chairman's conference room to wait while he finished a telephone conversation in his private office. She asked whether I would "like the fire turned on" because of the damp chill in the air. I said I didn't think so. After she left I looked around for a fireplace that I almost knew was not there, and found that the fire she referred to was an electric heater plugged into a wall receptacle.

In a very few minutes my friend hurried in with his usual cordial greeting and cheerful welcome. What had started many years before with a difficult and quite important business deal rather gradually developed into a comfortable friendship. His speech always reflected his education in the best English schools. As ever, his clothing was conservative and handsomely tailored. His hair was graying and thinning, as mine was too, even though he was some ten or twelve years younger than I was. He was extraordinarily wealthy, having inherited much money and then having built up a fortune of his own.

As soon as we decently could we began our business discussion, which was quite involved and complex. Each of us used notes we had prepared in advance, as reminders of points to be decided. Time passed. The secretary quietly opened the door to ask whether we would need files or anything before she would go out to lunch.

My host asked which I would prefer, going to the club for lunch or having a bite brought in for us to eat while we continued our meeting. My choice was what I knew he would prefer, to stay in the office and to finish our work. He knew how much I like smoked salmon from Scotland, so he asked his secretary to order that for both of us. I am not sure when or whether that little Miss Embray went out for her lunch, but I know she would not trust anyone else to serve our lunch to us. When she brought it in, it was colorful and delicious, It was salad, that incomparable sliced salmon, side dishes and a choice of sweets for dessert. This "bite" proved to be one of the very best meals I have had in London before or since, served in that old, uniquely English environment. As I sat there enjoying everything, I thought how my friend reflected so well the best in successful, civilized British character. In all ways, that is, except one. He was not British. He was the founder and almost sole owner of one of the most profitable shipping empires in Athens. He was one of the five or six most feared and hated, and above all else envied, ship owners known all over the world, as the "Golden Greeks".

ASSOCIATED LIVING

(W. Umbreit)

I have received a postcard from the Publishers Clearing House which says that, except for a few formalities, I am the winner of a $21 million "Super-prize." I am certainly glad to see this. My life has been spent, not in poverty, but mostly on the border. A thousand or two one way or another would keep me solvent or otherwise. However, now that I have these millions I have another problem. Of course, the government will take a third so I will be left with "only" about 16 million. It is reasonable for the government to take this since they are protecting me from fraud if not from downright theft.

But what am I to do with the 16 million left? If I take a million to give to charities, and lawyers (can I get by on so little? I will try) I still have 15 million left. I wish to invest this in something worthwhile, profitable, and which is likely to increase in value in the future so that the modest investment of 15 million can grow into a reasonable fortune and my descendants can associate with the really elite rich, something I never did, and which I am not sure that I would be able to do being somewhat naive and unmannered. But this would give them a chance I never had. I am not sure that all this money will do them any good and they may become "playboys" or worse, and I am not sure that association with the very rich builds the necessary character. They may well lose all the money I leave them so I want to invest it in an ever expanding profitable business. It's too late to invest in computers and besides I don't know anything about them (not that other investors really did).

I think that one should invest in a business that he knows something about. After careful investigation, I propose to establish a new kind of 'for profit' insane asylum. Looking at my contemporaries I think that this will be an expanding business in the future. Certainly several of my acquaintances seem to be on the verge of requiring such a place, if they are not already over the line. This business can only expand as the population (not too sane to start with) grows older and lives longer.

Of course, to be profitable we will have to charge large fees. And as such we need to cater to the rich. Not the very, very rich. They are too used to being catered to so that they would be impossible to deal with. Nor do we want to set up an asylum for the government types. They already have one in the Bureau of

Pensions and in the United Nations. But something on a little more modest scale, like a large luxurious country club, for example. We could, in fact, call it "Club Exquisite" to distinguish it from more modest establishments called "Retirement Homes" or "Communities for the Aging" or sometimes designated as the "rich man's poor house".

The inmates we would call "residents" or "club members" and, of course, they have complete control over their own lives. They can vote on and choose whatever they like, within certain limits, of course, and we set the limits. Of course, as management, we don't have to pay any attention, except to issue soothing statements at appropriate intervals which explain that we are looking into the matter. We can rely on the oldest rule of management, i.e., "What do they know about it?" and "How much stock do they hold?" And "Have they (or their lawyers) paid their fees on time?" This is the critical issue.

We propose that our club be organized into several sections. In one, the rooms would simulate a ship's stateroom, and one would look out from a simulated balcony onto scenes of the sea projected on the surrounding wall. One has dinner with the captain every third night and one simulates a sea cruise, without the sea sickness, of course. We can even have 'shore excursions' to shopping malls etc. We think that this would be very popular especially among the dowagers and those who used to love to travel.

In another section we would have a simulated stock exchange. There would be two, one for the bears where the stock is always going down so it can be purchased at the very lowest prices. Another for the bulls, where the stock is always going up. We can arrange it so the winnings or losses are set off against the monthly fee, the charge for this service being exactly the amount of market gain or loss. This is a very popular method called "creative accounting" and seems to be used by the very best and largest companies.

We would also have an indoor golf course, with a "Golf Club", or "course". There could be projections on the walls giving the impression that one was outdoors, and there can be regulated golf carts etc. moving about it. Many "club members" really don't want to go out into the sun too much so they can play here. We will use a soft ball (so there will be no damage if they accidentally hit each other) and there will be a magnet in the ball that is attracted to the hole so that "holes in one" are reasonably frequent and are always a source of celebration (which permits us to administer the necessary tranquilizers, required by ex-golfers, without ostentation).

Incidentally, we also use simulated silver (made of plastics) for eating so that members, if they attack each other, do little harm. We will also hold discussion groups. These latter are rather interesting. Since nobody listens, the members can all talk at the same time and make their arguments more pointed. We cannot, by law, restrain any of our members in any way, we cannot even use high rails on the beds (the lawmakers were evidently never in such an asylum, but we expect them shortly). And we will have wheel chairs with magnetic cushions to prevent too much spontaneous rising.

In short, we will make life as desirable and as expensive as possible. We have two innovations. One, we have found a way around the law that says you cannot commit a relative. And we allow no member to leave the grounds unless accompanied by his or her lawyer. This system would, we think, work very well. Before the funds come rolling in, we will have to make an initial capital investment of something more than the 15 million available. We intend to renovate an available nursing home when one suitable for this project becomes available and we think that the fifteen million backup would permit the borrowing of further funds to make this one of the best 'Associated Living' homes in the country. Watch for our announcements.

WEI-CHENG

(J. Wicks)

Wei-Cheng was in a rut. He would have been quick to admit that it was really a rather comfortable rut, and certainly he had no plans for removing himself from it, but still it was a rut. He was taller than most Chinese, about six feet tall, and sturdy in build, recalling several years of intense basketball playing in a college in mid-western United States, where he found sports much more interesting than acquiring his degree in chemical engineering. Like many other youths, indifferent depositories of useless information and never-to-be-used skills, he was scholastically prepared for a career in which he was destined never to work or to earn his living. He had a broad, clean-shaven, typically oriental face which occasionally brightened quite handsomely when he smiled. His features were regular, and his hair was coarse and very black. His posture was good. His compulsory service in the army in Taiwan before coming to the U.S. consisted of two years in the military police, not particularly enjoyable, but in some ways maturing. The rut he was in was his position as technician in the research department of an old and prosperous manufacturer, where his duties were routine, never stimulating, and were not in any way related to chemistry. He was only mildly bored.

Then by the kind of sheer accident that people always recall as brilliant planning, he came to the attention of an elderly executive in his company, and everything changed from routine to interesting and demanding and important. The executive who arranged the change in Wei-Cheng's life was thin and gaunt, which made him look taller than he was. His thinning hair of a nondescript gray color was combed straight back as if in retreat from his receding hairline. He was strict and firm and acutely ambitious. It was often hard to know whether his normally somber expression heralded deep concentration or just chronic bewilderment.

Wei-Cheng was quietly maneuvered out of research and into international marketing, specializing in the Far East area. He was trained and groomed and quite thoroughly pressured until he could be assigned to technical and marketing development with emphasis on, of all places, Taiwan. The young man felt, and now and then mentioned, a sense of gratitude for having been spirited out of the rut of research. And additionally, a surprising friendship developed among the two men and their wives. A sort of fringe benefit beyond helping the youth and selfishly solving a problem for the older one.

The Chinese New Year celebration in Taiwan is principally a family festival. Of course, there are street parades and the noise of clanging cymbals and fireworks, but the essence of the holiday is the gathering of families on New Year's Eve for dinner and reunion, with the oldest members of each family being the undisputed center of attention and respect. New Year's Eve is not a time for entertaining foreigners, but for the intimacy of assembled families.

Wei-Cheng and his elderly boss arranged an extensive Far East business trip so that they, and their wives, would be in Taiwan for technical discussions and corporate entertaining before the New Year holiday. Then after the celebration they would travel on to Bangkok for more business activity. The four were oddly assorted, two young, bright Orientals and two aging but still active Americans, and they had gradually become firm friends.

Early on the day before New Year's Day, Wei-Cheng relayed a message from his parents to his boss, a dignified invitation to spend New Year's Eve with the family in their Taipei home. It was unusual for outsiders, especially non-Orientals, to be included in the traditional celebration. But the invitation was not only cordial but almost insistent, so it was accepted, even though with some misgivings.

The house was modest in size, quite like all the other houses in the equally modest street in the outskirts of Taipei. All the houses faced directly on the narrow sidewalk. There were no yards and no trees, just a maximum number of decent dwellings fitted into the available space. Taipei is an incredibly crowded city.

Inside, the furnishings were rather sparse by American or English standards, but entirely adequate and scrupulously clean. The furniture was substantial, of the dark, almost black wood the Chinese call camphor wood, which is so indestructible that articles are passed from one generation of a family to the next. The walls were plain, with no picture, no mirrors. The largest room was not the living room, but the dining room. By the use of some ingenuity more than one table had been combined under the table cloths, and an assortment of chairs had been assembled to accommodate the family and guests for the holiday dinner.

Two Caucasians and twelve Orientals could make an unbalanced, rather awkward group. The host and hostess spoke no English, or, if they could, they refrained rather than risking the embarrassment of mistakes. They relied on their son as interpreter. Wei—Cheng's two younger brothers and a dear, shy adolescent sister with a low threshold of giggles understood as much English as they were learning in high school, which was not very useful. But some friendly hospitality can be extended with an absolute minimum of conversation; for example, Wei-Cheng's father and the old American exchanging toasts with the mercifully small glasses of a fiery Chinese distillate which compensates in potency for what it lacks in smoothness. The two Americans were made to feel comfortable and accepted, not curiosities to be watched with amusement.

Dinner was leisurely, with the usual numerous oriental courses and the very best of every type of food and Formosa tea. It was a happy meal for a loving family and for their guests so far from home. The meal ended at some time close to eleven o'clock. Conversation tapered off into a comfortable quiet.

All the diners left the huge table and went into the living room, and stood near the walls of the room. The patriarch of the family, Wei-Cheng's father, slowly and carefully arranged some small flowers on a wall shelf somewhat higher than eye level where there was a faded photograph of an ancient Chinese man. It was a picture of Wei-Cheng's paternal grandfather, long since dead, in mainland China. Then, with no apparent trace of self-consciousness, the patriarch knelt on the floor facing the shelf, and he seemed to be absorbed in silent contemplation. Then he prostrated himself with his forehead touching the floor. After a few moments, he quietly rose. Nobody said anything.

Later, when conversation was resumed before the two Americans departed during the din of fireworks through the city, they mentioned that they intended to visit the Nationalist Chinese Museum while they were in Taipei, to see an exhibit of classic Chinese calligraphy. Wei-Cheng's father said, through his interpreter son, that he was an amateur calligrapher and he would write to his American guest in his own writing style, for Wei-Cheng to provide the translation. The New Year's Eve dinner party ended with a sense of respect and friendly comfort obviously shared by all fourteen people of varied ages, races, and backgrounds. The promised letter in calligraphy arrived later. It was four pages but unfortunately it does not reproduce well on the computer. Here is its translation.

Taipei, Taiwan
September 4, 1972

Dear Mr. Wicks:

I have received and read both of your letters with sincere gratitude. I felt joyful and blessed by your honorable presence during your last visit to my humble home.

I do not deserve your thanks for those simple dishes. It was merely a token of friendship from the host. As a matter of our culture and custom, the Chinese always treat their honored guests with the best wine and food. Three thousand years ago our foremost prophet, Confucius once said, "What joy it is to have a friend from afar yonder!" Among the Chinese moral and ethical standards, friendship is one of the five codes which we have always kept in mind. The affectionate communications between friends can enhance mutual discussion and encouragement.

The family and I are proud of the

fact that Wei-Cheng is working with you for the same company. But Wei-Cheng is still inexperienced and unpolished in many ways. I hope you will teach him, guide him so he will be steered in the right course.

Please forgive me that I did not answer your letter at once. That is because I wanted to write to you personally and my hopeless English stopped me from doing that. Instead, I have written in my own language for Wei-Cheng to translate it into English to extend to you my sincere thanks and utmost admiration from a place afar.

The season has stepped into deep Fall and the temperatures turn cooler. Hope you will take care of yourself.

My best regards to Madame Wicks.

Sincerely,
Lung, Tien Wu

It might be natural enough to envision the kindly Confucian host and calligrapher as an artistic, sensitive, elderly Chinese of slight build, perhaps a former school teacher or civil servant. That would be a mistake. His gentle hospitality was concealed by his appearance. He was tall, muscular, solid, a native of Hunan Province which is famous for big, raw-boned men and women. He was scarred by many violent battles against communist hordes which overran mainland China years before. Whenever he was not speaking or smiling, his expression was severe and stern. It was the face of a man well acquainted with suffering and struggle in the tragic and world-respected army of Generalissimo (and later President of Nationalist China) Chiang Kai Shek. The host calligrapher had retired with the rank of General.

MEMORIES OF JERUSALEM
(W. Umbreit)

Recently I was involved in a conversation which recalled to me memories of Jerusalem as it was 30 years ago. I always stayed at the Intercontinental Hotel perched on the Mount of Olives. The Israeli's do not like this hotel because it was built with Arab money and during the time that Jordan occupied the area, the city, and especially the roads, were shelled by Jordanian troops. But the view from the hotel is unsurpassed—so much history, and religion, and conflict have occurred in the area covered by the view.

Thirty years ago, the people were very friendly. Once, at the Wailing Wall, a bar mitzvah was in progress and as just passing strangers, my wife and I were invited to it, and we shared the refreshments. Another time, on a Saturday, my wife and I took a stroll through the orthodox Jewish quarter. No cars are allowed, ever, and there are posts down the middle of the road to prevent them from entering. Since it was a day of worship, the streets, normally very full, were practically empty. It was in December and it had just rained; water was still standing in the streets. As we were walking along, a man emerged from one of the buildings, addressed us in English and asked if we would like to attend a service at the synagogue. We declined on the ground that we were so unfamiliar with the Jewish services that we would be bound to make some embarrassing mistake.

But the very fact that he invited us struck me as unusual and touching. Have you ever invited a stranger passing your church, to come in and worship?

Arabs and Jews got along pretty well. We particularly noted an orthodox Jew in full regalia who had walked from the orthodox Jewish quarter through the bustling Arab quarter to reach the wailing wall, there to conduct his worship and had returned the same way, without being once molested, shouted at, insulted or, in fact, probably even noticed.

One other item is unusual. Throughout the Middle East, guns were strictly forbidden, except in Israel. All citizens, Jews or Arab, served an obligatory time in the army. But in Israel they were allowed to carry their weapons and one might board a bus with maybe 30 people aboard of which 4 or 5 would be soldiers with rifles. They even took them to worship. The army itself was in evidence, but that did not mean that it was actively patrolling the streets or keeping watch on the citizens. It was mostly young people coming to the training camps or going home from them or going out to get lunch etc. One did not get the feeling of danger, but rather of cooperation.

NUMBERS
(J. Wicks)

Starting at the age of about three years, most of us use numbers practically every day for the rest of our lives. We use them for measuring, keeping score, buying, selling, paying bills, earning a living and yet there may be some features about numbers that are overlooked. In fact, they may be interesting or even amusing if we look at them closely. Mathematicians, statisticians and actuaries, a rather solemn and serious-minded lot, they always seem to me, hardly ever mention numbers themselves as being fun to observe.

Just as an example, look at a small series of consecutive numbers we use over and over again: 1,2,3,4,5,6,7 and 8. Starting at the left side, the first two digits are the number twelve, which equals the product of multiplying the third digit by the fourth, (3x4); and the fifth and sixth digits are fifty-six, which equals the product of multiplying the seventh digit by the eighth, (7x8). Not spectacular, but try to find any other group of consecutive numbers which can do the same!

NUMBERS ONE THROUGH EIGHT

1 and	2 together	=	12
3 times	4	=	12
5 and	6 together	=	56
7 times	8	=	56

Some other consecutive numbers are also worth examining. Look for the moment at all the numbers from 1 to 15, and you will notice that 1+2=3, and 4+5+6 = 7+8, and 9+10+11+12 = 13+14+15.

NUMBERS ONE THROUGH FIFTEEN

$1 + 2 = 3$

$4 + 5 + 6 = 15$

$7 + 8 \quad\quad = 15$

$9 + 10 + 11 + 12 = 42$

$13 + 14 + 15 \quad\quad = 42$

Number One

And we should not overlook number 1 and occasionally repeated series of 1. Considering consecutive ascending numbers from 1 to 9, followed by descending numbers from 8 to 1, we see 12345678987654321. The square root of that rather impressive number is 111,111,111.

Number Nine

Of course it is not only the first eight digits that are interesting. Number 9 has some unique features of its own. For example, if we multiply any number by 9, and add the digits of the resulting number, the sum will be 9.

NUMBER NINE

9 x 5 = 45	Digits 4 + 5 = 9
9 x 17= 153	1 + 5 + 3 = 9
9 x 24= 216	2 + 1 + 6 = 9
9 x any number	digits added = 9

If we reverse the digits of the result of multiplying any number by 9, the number we produce will be an exact multiple of 9. (Try it).

Then too, we can select any number we like, and divide it by 9. The remainder we obtain will be the same as the remainder we get by adding the digits of the number we have selected and dividing this by 9. This may sound a little complicated but look at the examples below.

RANDOM NUMBERS WITH NINE

		Remainder
258	divided by 9 = 28.666	0.666
2 + 5 + 8 = 15	9 = 1.666	0.666
6371	divided by 9 = 708.888	0.888
6 + 3 + 7 + 1	9 = 1.888	0.888

We can choose any two-digit number and multiply it by 9. We can then add the digits of the resulting number. They will always be 9 or an exact multiple of 9. (Try it).

Perhaps it is only coincidence that the number to dial on the telephone in Great Britain for emergency assistance is 999. And mentioning Great Britain, large numbers there are not all the same as we use here in the U.S. Here, a thousand thousands are a million, and a thousand millions are a billion. But in Great Britain it requires a million millions to make a billion. Billionaires over there are quite scarce.

Thirteen

One number that has been given a bad name for centuries is the number 13. Some hotels count their floors as 11,12,14,15, etc. just to avoid having a thirteenth floor which superstitious guests would refuse to occupy. Thirteen has been blamed for some disasters it could never have caused. And Friday, the 13th has been regarded as a day of ill luck. Yet 13 is a number which is capable of some interesting behaviors in square calculations, in square roots, and even in complete reversal of the numerical order of the digits. For example if we square 13 (multiply 13 by 13) we obtain the number 169. If we reverse the order of the digits we get 961. The square root of 961 is 31. And if we reverse these digits we are back to 13!

THIRTEEN
13 x 13 =169   reverse digits=961
Whose square root is 31 (31X31= 961)
Reverse digits of 31=13

And adding the digits of 169 (13 squared) we obtain 16. Adding the digits of 13 we get 4 which is the square root of 16.

One rather undistinguished number, 153, appeals to the arithmetic enthusiasts because if they cube all three digits and add the results, they get the same number.

ONE HUNDRED FIFTY THREE
1 x 1 x 1 =   1
5 x 5 x 5 = 125
3 x 3 x 3 =   27
          Sum   153

Mathematicians have concentrated for generations on extremely complex problems in technical subjects most people have never ever heard about, including number theory. We can't balance our checkbooks with quadratic remainders, or with Fibonacci series, but we can, and do, use common ordinary numbers every day of our lives.

There is nothing new or original or spectacular about any of these comments about numbers, but isn't it pleasant to remind ourselves that numbers themselves can be interesting, even fun, if we observe them closely.

WHAT'S LEFT?

(J. Wicks)

It seems a little strange to me,
That dreams of what I'd like to be
Are gone- no telling where they
went.
The wishes closest to my heart
Were first and fastest to depart;
What's left? A very small percent.

WRITERS

(J. Wicks)

Two men I have known and liked for many years had a lifelong ambition in common but they never became acquainted with each other. Both wanted, urgently wished, to be writers. Both had above average intelligence, and had at least normal levels of education and background.

One man and I were friends for about sixty-five years until the end of his life. He knew even when he was a teenager that his ambition was to be a writer, and not just any kind of writer, but a journalist. I wondered many times how prominent a part in his decision may have been the dramatic and popular plays featuring the intensity of the street-smart, hard-driving newspaper reporter who proves to be heroic. But it doesn't matter now what motivated his lifelong ambition.

His education was appropriate for what he wanted to be. He studied journalism, of course, and here his story begins to unravel. I have no way of knowing how many newspaper jobs he sought, or how much effort he may have put into an intensive career search when he graduated. All I know is that he found no newspaper job then, and that he never wrote a single article or line for publication all the rest of his life.

The other jobs were always taken with the expectation that his career in journalism was temporarlly on hold. Whatever work he did was for the sensible purpose of avoiding starvation, and he did each job faithfully enough to be paid, but he saw himself as temporally employed, awaiting assignment as a journalist. In the meantime, he was too busy with work to do any writing.

As the years passed, I did not observe in him any developing awareness that his career was entirely different from his original plan. His relatives knew it, his friends realized it, but I believe he never quite relinquished the illusion that in some unspecified way he was going to become a successful newspaper writer. Inevitably, what he did was become an old man.

It is hard to review sensibly this old

friend's life or that portion of it during which we were well acquainted. He remained for some 30 years in a civil service job that could only charitably be termed dead-end. In it he earned his living, and a pension, and through a payroll deduction program, he accumulated enough money to pay his expenses during the last four or five years of his life. Then he had to accept the disappointment of realizing that he could not manage his own financial matters. He had never married. He had outlived all his relatives. Our many years of close friendship led to his decision to turn over to me the management of all his assets. Finally I was the one to make all funeral and burial arrangements and to pay his bills when my old friend died.

But something was missing. If we are all predestined in the ways we will live out our lives, perhaps he was programmed to stay out of even a single newspaper office in all his lifetime. Success or failure must surely be at least partly determined by whether we do or fail to do what we really want most urgently to do. As much as I liked my old friend, I think now that his working lifetime was a failure.

He wanted to write, but he didn't get around to it.

My other friend tried several different major subjects in college, finally settling at his family's insistence on architecture. The young graduate used architecture as a way to earn a living; sometimes quite prosperous and other times discouraging financially. But it was never what he really wanted to do. He wanted to write. And he did write some articles for technical publications even though there was often no greater reward than seeing his efforts published under his name. The absence of any fee or payment was provoking, but the satisfaction of writing for publication was still the motive for more essays and articles. As he grew old and physically infirm, his profession of architecture became too demanding; he retired.

But he still wrote. Articles, short stories, Op-ed contributions, whatever came to mind. He was impelled to write, and continued to write for years. Possibly he felt that eventually he could be published, but I really don't think that this was his major motivation. He wanted to write. There was something in his psyche which demanded expression and this desire could only be satisfied by writing. My friend wrote because he was impelled to do so. What he wrote is rather interesting, but he ran up against a difficulty faced by most writers. Publishers are interested in printing 'what will sell' and they employ editors and agents to select such works. As such they tend to select things that appeal to a large audience. After all, they have to print several hundred books and distribute them to bookstores. The initial investment is enormous and should the book not 'catch on', the losses can be large. At the time my friend was writing this was the situation. Today, with the advent of "print on demand" publishing and the use of computers, it would be quite likely that his work could have been published.

A fairly objective overview of this good friend's life, now that I have administered his estate, is somewhat confusing. Using conventional standards it was not much of a success, financially or professionally. But there are various forms of success. I know that he fell short of his real ambition which was to become a recognized and admired writer. I also know that he achieved the satisfying success of actually doing the very thing that meant the most to him-- putting into written form his thoughts and opinions and ambitions. Never mind how few people ever read his words. I may be the only one to think so, but I consider him a success.

He wanted to write, and he wrote.

POEMS

BACK PAIN

(J. Wicks)

> Sit straight in your chair!
> Keep your head in the air!
> I found that I just couldn't do it.
> But the pain went away,
> I'm happy to say.
> Diagnosis: I musta outgrew it.
>
> These are somewhat trying times,
> Hence I'll rhyme you no more rhymes.

ON BEING EIGHTY SOMETHING
(J. Wicks)

I have long thought of octogenarians as elderly remnants of life, usually deprived of useful strength and/or mental liveliness. They were people who had outlived actuarial age tables and had survived most of their generation peers. Now, over halfway through my eighties, I suddenly discover that I am one of those octogenarians, myself. And it is not as bad as I thought. It's worse.

Let's consider for a moment the subject of falling. Normal childhood and youth almost always will include falls in games, in careless hurrying, in tripping over obstacles. Very seldom do those youthful falls cause any more damage than a few bruises and dirty clothes. But in the eighties, falls reveal our vulnerability. Two falls in the past year or so injured first one wrist (right) then the other one (left) and sabotaged my self-confidence in walking. Four of my elderly neighbors and friends also broke bones in the uncomfortable time that my arms were decorated with casts.

Then there is the matter of meals. Never would I have believed that the time might come when many of my favorite foods would be on a list of restricted items, or worse yet, would become indigestible. At a time in life when dining can be unhurried and leisurely, permissible entrees are a Spartan few which become monotonous through constant repetition.

Also, while I was a young man for seventy-five years or so, I had the feeling, some might say an illusion, that I was needed to accomplish some worthwhile objectives. I guess I felt that most of my activities were productive. That pleasant sensation does not endure into the eighties. There is no illusion about being really needed or even likely to achieve any important activity. Another change is in memory. the reduction in memory seems to be almost a universal annoyance.

However, this list of old-age symptoms must not to be a recital of everything finally gone wrong. Just this morning I was reflecting on the many benefits and pleasures that are part of the phenomenon of growing old.

Problem is, now I can't remember any of them.

ON BEING NINETY SOMETHING
(J. Wicks)

Aug 14, 2002

In "ON BEING EIGHTY SOMETHING" I said "I *had long thought of octogenarians as elderly remnants of a life, usually deprived of useful strength and/or mental liveliness. They were people who had outlived actuarial age tables. Then, I suddenly discovered that I was one of those octogenarians myself. And it was not as bad as I thought. It was worse.*" But now at ninety it is somewhat different.

I said that falls, while causing little damage to the young, were difficult for those in their eighties. But in the nineties, falling reveals a real vulnerability. Two falls in the past few years injured first one wrist (right) and then the other (left) and sabotaged my self-confidence in walking. And during the uncomfortable time that my arms were decorated with casts or bandages, four of my elderly friends and neighbors also broke bones.

If the eighties revealed our vulnerability to falling, the nineties disclose the possibility that much more may go wrong. For example, another fall or two contributed a total of five fractures to my vertebrae. Among several recommended treatments, I spent eight weeks of bed rest in a "respite supervised" environment, not quite a hospital and not quite home either. I absorbed quantities of pain-suppressing medicine which did very little to relieve the pain but did contribute to clinical depression and a somewhat subdued view of the world. When I was in the eighties I might have luxuriated in self-pity. But at the age of 90 I no longer had that luxury. I could not just lie around, I had not the time for it. There was living to be done. Because I was too weak and too confused to walk alone, I agitated aggressively for return to my own home, for most of those eight weeks. I borrowed a walker from an old friend and learned how to walk all over again and thus proceeded gradually back into independent living. Not exactly entirely independent. All my life I have cleaned my apartment and washed my linens. Now that has been taken over by the housekeeping staff and I rather enjoy the freedom. But when one can overcome obstacles and get a little assistance, being ninety is not too bad.

In the nineties our appetites undergo some changes which accommodate the permissible variety of foods. Even though many items are restricted, the passing of years makes us acquainted with the foods we can properly handle. Foods which I would have avoided eight or ten years ago, are much more welcome now. Possibly the number and condition of our teeth may change our eating habits for the better, making us more satisfied. In my nineties I am eating better than in the seventies or eighties and I enjoy it.

At some time during my middle age, three people decided that they wanted me to handle their estates as executor of their wills. That required no particular effort or concentration from me, until all thee of them died within a short time and all three estates had to be administered within one year (as it happened a year into my eighties).

Now that these duties have all been completed, I am benefited by the experience, and I am substantially older. The result is that I am revising my own estate plan quite thoroughly. My financial assets are invested in ways that my executor will welcome, requiring simple handling. Everything else that I own is now undergoing a quiet review, with the acknowledgement that not all that I cherish will be of any interest to my heirs. Getting rid of old treasure can be a tiresome chore for any executor and I am determined to dispose of as much as possible while I am still alive.

Take books, for example. For years I accumulated and read and re-read books on a variety of subjects and, of course, I carefully kept them all. But now, what I cherish among my assortment of books can be of no interest to the younger generations of my family. In fact, they can be a heavy burden. So now in my nineties I am quietly inquiring about how to give them away where someone might welcome at least some of them.

When I wrote "On Being Eighty Something" I deplored the old-age symptom of forgetting so much of what we try to recall quickly. Of course it can be tantalizing to forget names and facts which we should be able to remember, and then later, without any conscious effort, to recall suddenly the name or word that has eluded us. Maybe what we lack is not exactly memory, it may be simply instant retrieval from the vast amount of mental storage stuff which we have accumulated in our lifetime.

As I sift through the recollections of ninety years, I suspect that it may be a merciful development that memory of some painful and disappointing intervals has faded and slipped away. In the nineties, some old-age memory lapses are not so bad, after all.

I can see a contrast between my thoughts recorded in "On Being Eighty Something" and my ideas now, about ten years later. Certainly there have been adjustments required as we have lived through our sixties and seventies and eighties, and those of us who are still alive, physically and mentally have accomplished most of those changes. I find it encouraging to reflect on the fact that most of the inevitable adjustments in our life style have made things better, not worse, for our nineties. For example, now I feel newly appreciative for the remaining family and friends I have, and for the everyday comforts of having what I need when I need it. I no longer deplore the losses which annoyed me ten or twenty years ago. My complaints in my eighties have subsided in importance, so I tend to ignore them.

I appreciate having lived longer today than any of my forebears ever lived. And I see now that it has been a rather interesting life, overcoming some serious difficulties and enjoying some very good luck.

About ten years ago, reaching the eighties, required that I learn to adapt. For me there was the shock of losing my wife, my home, my career activities, and the dependable part of my physical health. But I learned that adjustment and adaptation are entirely possible, mostly because the ability to adjust also increased with advancing age.

Looking back now at all that I thought and wrote "On Being Eighty Something", there was not much that I could claim was really good and favorable. Now that I consider and write thoughts on "Being Ninety Something", I realize that I am more comfortable, content, and better adjusted than I was ten or more years ago.

I hope to be able to write something much more interesting when I reach the age of one hundred.

ON BEING NINETY
(W. Umbreit)

Unlike my friend, Jack Wicks, I never wrote an essay on what it felt like to be eighty something. As a matter of fact, when I became 80 I was so immersed in countless problems that I simply did not have time for reflection. I could no longer manage my 9-room house and the three acres of lawn and garden that surrounded it. I had to move to a retirement home, which I was in the process of doing when I became 80. I often expound upon the observation that one should move into such institutions (of your choice, of course) before you absolutely have to so that you can adjust to the somewhat different way of life that they represent. But I moved because I had to, although I was vigorous enough to make the adjustments required without too much difficulty and have lived in reasonable contentment since. Now that I am ninety, what is life like?

I can still eat reasonably well. Food has not lost too much flavor although it does tend to taste much the same. I only eat one meal a day at noon, and just very small supper and a cup of coffee for breakfast. If I eat more I tend to become overly fat. This is partly due to the fact that I take no exercise to speak of. I suffer from the permanent effects of 'shingles" which is called 'post herpetic neuralgia" and for which there is no known treatment or cure. For me, even pain-killing narcotics don't work. It therefore is somewhat painful for me to exercise so I don't do it. As they may say, I am as lazy as one can get.

I can read, but it is increasingly difficult to do so. And while I used to enjoy reading and read at least two books a week, now it takes me a week or more to read one.

But I do have a compensation, I have learned how to use the computer and perhaps spend 3-4 hours a day on it. It provides not only communication with my friends, but also is, in effect, a large library right at my desktop. The only thing really wrong is that there is such an enormous amount of information (not all of it reliable) that I am sure that I cannot assimilate even a small fraction of it in the time I have left. The present generation, being familiar with computers, will have no difficulties, but many of the people living here want to have 'nothing to do' with computers. And here is one of the effects of age. We cannot remember anything for very long, a matter of minutes, sometimes. We are given instructions for the computer, and we do the procedure successfully, and five minutes later we have no idea how we did it.

Complaints--complaints. Isn't there anything good about becoming 90? I'm thinking--I'm thinking. Well, I sleep well. From about 11 to 7 and then in the afternoon either from 1:30 to 3 or from 3:30 to 5. This is good for me, but some people can't sleep and I feel sorry for them. Sleeping potions don't work, all one can do (reading is too difficult at that time of night) is play solitaire or free card on the computer. Also there seems to be no urgency about getting things done. I do not have to worry about my career and how it is being hijacked. So long as I get my retirement check I can live, if not blissfully, at least adequately. And if I don't get the check, there is a business office that will investigate it for me. There must be some other good things, maybe I will remember.

Did you ever notice how nobody really listens? This becomes more evident as one ages. If one listens to the conversations between us oldsters, one finds the two or more individuals each talking about their own interests and paying little or no attention to what was said to them. You get used to this. My wife had to live in a 'healthcare facility'; essentially a hospital without the surgical patients. Here I used to talk with a very pleasant man, but it disturbed me that I could make no sense of what he was saying. I then realized that he could make no sense of what I said. So we had nice conversations neither of us understanding the other. One night he refused to go to bed. He said that he had bet on the races and won and he would not go to bed until he had been paid his winnings. I asked him how much? He said that he had won $1.67 so I paid him the $ 1.67 and he went to bed peaceably.

When I was younger (above) I was firmly of the opinion that one never had a new idea after the age of 35, which seemed to be really old. That is not at all true. Even today I have new ideas, such as putting the picture of my sister holding me (above). I am not sure that these are necessarily **good** ideas but ideas they are. I'm not sure that one should keep an open mind, too much might leak out, but I think one should be willing to let things in, if they are not too absurd, and are worth thinking about.

Some more! "There goes that doddering idiot" may be 50% right. Doddering we do, we can't help it. It is a real problem. One can put one's feet out to walk but they don't go to a spot which helps maintain balance. We 'dodder'. Sometimes this gets so bad that we can't walk unassisted and we must use a cane or walker, or even an electric cart. It seems to be inevitable with age, we see it all around us here, even in people who seem to be in vigorous health. Just watch them get up from a table--the first few steps will be uncertain even if they eventually recover. It may strike one anytime and it is a real nuisance. Idiots we may become but hopefully not yet.

Then there is hearing. We gradually lose it. There are all sorts of hearing aids, expensive little things that fit into the ear. They do help some, but tend to amplify the wrong sounds. They enhance the clatter of silverware but not the human voice to the same extent. As such, many in their 90s do not hear well. They shout at one another, which works sometimes, but really drives one with a hearing aid turned on to become deaf due to the noise. There is back pain, and muscle pain, and stiff joints. And as we age we tend to hump over. Just look at us. Then, we cannot bend over enough to tie our shoes or put on socks. It becomes a real chore. Just listing these miserable things that happen to us makes one wonder why we continue.

I think that it is something within our soul. It is not usually fear of death. If you ask among us, most will say they are ready to go, but hope that it will come suddenly and that it will not be a slow lingering time. But there is still the sun to be seen, and the rain, and the green grass. There is the sound of birds and the sight and smell of flowers. There are still the bonds of friends and family and the sense of participating in an ongoing drama of which we are still a part. So while I cannot describe an ever improving life to be had at ninety, I can say that not all is despair—there are good things too. After all there are good days and bad days. I had a good day last Thursday.

But there is a condition here. As things become increasingly difficult; when bending down and getting up become real chores—one could use a more pungent term—one must increasingly resist the option of giving in to them. One must have the courage, the persistence, indeed, the complete arrogance to feel that one will not give in to these problems, not surrender one's life to a series of constantly recurring difficulties. As Hamlet says one should take up arms against a sea of troubles and by opposing, defeat them. This is what one must do to live at the age of ninety, or at least to live a tolerable life. If one does not, then one becomes a mere repository of complaint and resignation, as we see in some our acquaintances. To resist this barrage of difficulties, it is helpful to have something to do. Raise flowers, carve wood figures, write essays, paint pictures, photograph daily scenes, explore the world with the computer internet, discuss (not merely read) written works, or write them yourself. Maybe this writing is for just that very purpose. While golf or tennis or baseball may no longer be possible for you to play, you can discuss them with like minded individuals. When I first came to this place, I was introduced to a group of three elderly men at a dining room table. After exchanging names we ate in silence. Finally it appeared that there was a baseball strike and they had nothing to talk about. The point is, not that this is absurd, but that conversation about a subject that means, or once meant, much to you, and recitation of experiences and sharing experiences and memories with others with a like interest, provided a purpose to their lives and helped them to oppose the deterioration of the physical well-being. So do something that will occupy you, keep you interested, and let you think of things other than your difficulties. And thus you will find something good in becoming ninety. I promised not to preach, but it did me some good, so you don't have to listen.

REMEMBRANCES OF SEOUL
(J. Wicks)

In those days in the mid 1970's, Kimpo Airport in Seoul, Korea was noisy, poorly lighted, practically unventilated, and reeking from the smoke of cheap Korean cigarettes and garlic. Numerically there always seemed to be enough employees, but processing the routine functions of incoming and departing travelers took much longer than it should require. Viewed realistically, it was a dreary place.

One elderly arrival leaving the baggage claim area looked weary and rumpled after his long flight on Korea Airlines from Anchorage to Seoul. His eyes were bloodshot and irritated. Impatience and annoyance and fatigue showed in his expression, even in his slumping posture. John Wagner was nearly ready for his impending retirement. Of course he is much older now, if he is still alive. And if he has survived, he quite likely may have forgotten that day when he felt the burden of too many years of responsibility plus eight or ten hours of travel discomfort.

Younger and more vigorous passengers reached the windows of arrival-passport clerks before Wagner, so a line of people was ahead of him, moving slowly. He placed his luggage on the floor and moved it ahead with one foot each time the line advanced. A heavy woman in a business suit was next in line behind him. Twice she bumped him with the oversized carry-on bag slung over her shoulder.

Then, when he finally approached the passport clerk's window, Wagner silently slid his passport across the desk surface to the clerk, who glanced at it and shoved it back with just two words in English, "No visa!" Exasperated, the weary traveler explained that no visa was required for the three days he would be in Seoul, and he showed the entrance and exit rubber stamp impressions on his passport from previous trips, all without Korean visas. The clerk took the passport and disappeared, for a long discussion with another clerk. When he returned he was sullen. He placed the date stamp on a fresh page of the passport with exaggerated slowness. Everything took too long. The woman next in line behind Wagner swore.

At the taxi lane there was only one available vehicle remaining. It was an old small sedan operated by an ancient driver. He was short and light of build, with unusually deep creases in the skin of his face and forehead. There was an intensity about his expression, especially in his eyes, as he looked closely at Wagner, almost as if deciding whether to accept him as a passenger. Instinct alerted John Wagner that this was a shrewd, hard old man, possibly and quite likely dishonest. But there was no choice, so he allowed the driver to put the luggage into the car trunk. The driver either could not speak a word of English or would not try.

The taxi was dirty. A candy wrapper and a crumpled empty cigarette package were on the seat. Part of a newspaper was on the floor. The passenger lowered himself awkwardly into the back seat. He spoke the only Korean words he had ever bothered to learn: "Cho Sun",which was the name of the only top quality hotel in Seoul in the mid-70's.

The driver muttered something unintelligible. He started the motor, stalled it twice, then started it again, raced the engine and lurched the car out into the traffic lane. When he flipped on the switch of the fare meter it rushed into a noisy impatient chattering as it registered digits in Korean won.

At best in those years the ride into downtown Seoul was rather long and uncomfortable. But this time it was going to be much longer, because the taxi was not going gradually lower into the Han River valley by the usual route to center city. It was snarling through its lower gears, climbing much higher up a steep rough-surfaced hillside road. Wagner was not only tired and uncomfortable, but suddenly and thoroughly angry. All he could shout at the driver was still: "Cho Sun! Cho Sun!" And the driver nodded

129

slightly and continued driving up the mountain road. The passenger was seething, but there was nothing he could do about it, even if the taxi continued to go up and down mountain roads for the rest of the day.

An obvious trick to increase the taxi fare many times over, and wasting time. Greed, taking advantage of a defense-less foreigner. A disgusting old crook, as Wagner had suspected at first sight. A tiresome plane trip, the fatigue, the stupid delay with the passport clerk, and now a thoroughly hateful wretch driving up a remote mountain road far removed from the normal route leading to center city.

Something was added to all the dis-comforts; sheer anger. The old taxi was now growling up the steep grade in low gear, moving with tantalizing slowness. After what seemed like an endless climb, ahead was a cleared space at the left side of the road, big enough for just one car, but now unoccupied. The driver pulled into the clearing and shut off the motor. Now what, a hold-up?

Still without a spoken word, the driver pointed to the view down into the valley. Wagner learned, probably too late in life to do him much good, how abruptly anger can be transformed into a couple of entirely different emotions. Looking down into the Han River valley, he could suddenly see why he had been taken toward his destination by a much longer, unusual route.

He saw the main road which led to center city. All traffic was at a standstill, paralyzed by dozens of cars and trucks in line, bumper to bumper, stopped by two police cars, their lights flashing, positioned across the road. A massive dirty brown cloud of smoke was spreading in all directions. The oldest and poorest section of the city was in flames in what the newspapers the next morning would describe as the worst fire in the history of Seoul.

Perhaps I should mention that I, Jack Wicks, was the elderly irritable traveler in these notes and that John Wagner was a name I invented. Did you ever guess?

TRAVEL

(J. Wicks)

> You zip across the ocean
> at a speed that's supersonic.
> It's just great.
> But with customs in slow motion
> and with traffic that's moronic,
> You're still late.

HOTELS

(J. Wicks)

It is strange, the recollections and impressions that will remain with a traveler long after the days of travel are ended. Consider hotels, for example. For people far away from home, especially on frequent and extended business trips, hotels become a fairly important part of life. And years after the experiences, little fragments of recall can still cause a frown or a smile or just a twinge of nostalgia.

One pointless recollection that still comes back is about the Meridien Hotel in Cairo. It was located on the very edge of the Nile, with all guest rooms facing the river. That was accomplished by building the hotel high and wide, but only deep enough for a room and a wide hallway. There were no rooms facing the side away from the river. Each large and comfortable room had a small porch, with a table and a couple of chairs occupying practically all the porch area.

Each time I stayed there I followed the same routine of ordering breakfast before going to sleep at night, always asking for room service at or near seven in the morning. When the waiter arrived, more or less on time, I asked him to place the tray on my porch table. Then every morning I sat in comfort on the porch to eat breakfast, watching the endless traffic of small and medium-size boats going up and down the Nile, nearly all relying only on sails for power. It was quiet. Mornings were almost always comfortably cool, even though temperatures would soar to stifling heat a few hours later. What is it that brings that recollection back so clearly, I wonder? Perhaps it is the remembering of a sense of calm, of well-being, early in the day, before becoming involved in business pressures. I have nearly forgotten frustrating discussions with the U.S. Embassy in Cairo, and difficult negotiations with canny Egyptian entrepreneurs, and the everlasting heat and noise and air pollution of that beloved and detested city, but I recall clearly the relaxed and comfortable breakfast time on my tiny porch, looking affectionately at the Nile, and across the river at the bustling early traffic of cars and trucks starting for a busy day.

And then there is the Grand Hotel in Taipei, Taiwan. A luxury hotel built and owned by the independently wealthy wife of Generalissimo Chiang Kai-Shek, it reflected perfect Chinese taste and dignity in every respect. But I don't especially think now about the tremendous lobby, or the beautiful dining room with many small private dining rooms adjoining it on three sides, or the massive carved wooden furniture in every guest room, or even the impeccable service.

I think now of a day that we checked out about mid-morning, leaving to travel to Hong Kong and from there to Bangkok, Thailand. It was during the busiest season, with all hotel rooms booked well in advance. As I checked out, many incoming guests were gathered around the reception desks, clamoring for rooms that had not yet even been vacated or cleaned. The clerical staff was courteous and efficient, but under obvious pressure.

When we arrived at the airport we cleared passport control and ticket validation on the ground floor of the huge terminal building, then we went on the twin escalators on the long ride to the second floor where arrival and departures were located, along with the waiting room, offices, and restaurants and shops.

Near the top of the escalator a porter's overloaded baggage cart slipped out of control and struck my wife Phoebe's leg just below the knee. She cried out in pain and panic. I made her as comfortable as possible on a long wooden bench, applied a plastic bag of ice cubes obtained from the restaurant, and went in search of a doctor.

In the next hour or so we had a careful examination by a Chinese airport physician, a series of x—ray pictures, bandaging, and a complete change of plans. A plane trip to Hong Kong was impossible. A room to stay another night in Taipei was out of the question at the height of the season with all hotels over-booked.

I made one telephone call, almost without hope. I called the Grand Hotel, explained that Phoebe had been injured in an accident in the airport and asked whether they could possibly help me to find a room for the night in any decent hotel in Taipei. They told me to come back at once to the Grand Hotel. When we arrived, a wheel chair was ready for our use, we were shown to the same room we had vacated that morning, and we were welcomed warmly.

What I remember most clearly, though, is that there was a large bowl of beautiful red roses on the coffee table, with a 'get-well' card for Madame Wicks.

HOW TO CHOOSE WORDS

(W. Umbreit)

Like many in my generation, I use the computer and find many of its properties to be useful. Fortunately I learned to type in High School some 70 years ago. Yet I don't really quite trust the computer. Every once in a while, especially after visits from my grandchildren, some folder or file or program shows up whose function I do not know, whose language (from Bangladesh?) I cannot make out. Where it came from and how it got there is a mystery to me. Recently I found such a folder labeled Baffle, and since I was baffled I clicked on it and got six files one of which, called Bghelp, showed as its icon a book with a question mark on it. Clicking on it I got a page that said that the program involved was called Baffle Gab and that given a noun, for example, the program would invent an adverb and adjective which would appropriately modify it. And thus we could all "colloquialise with deftness and style". That sounded good; deftness and style were what I needed. Indeed, I found it very useful.

In the following I have underlined the words the computer provided to modify the word I gave it, so you can see how much style can be added to ordinary conversation. Since it was on my mind, I started with "style". I found that I could get an <u>empemrally genotypical</u> style or a <u>quantiatively arcane</u> style or a <u>episodicaly compendirus</u> style (and I gather about 50 more). Doesn't that sound better than just little old "style"? Your friends, and especially your <u>luculent</u> enemies, will be amazed. Where did this idiot learn such important and <u>resounding compendious</u> words? And they will not question you too closely since it would only show that their <u>expedientially barbarous</u> education or <u>qualitatively exigent</u> memory, or more likely both, were <u>quasi exponablely</u> deficient.

I wish I could tell you how to get to this program. I don't know its HTML (whatever that means). When I went to the web with "baffle.com" I got three articles only. One said that the police in Salt Lake City were baffled. A second, called "Advice for the Baffled" appeared to me (being inexperienced in these matters) to be semi pornographic nonsense. And the third detailed some baffled crops in a valley in Utah. The Web, I am told, is very useful in broadening your knowledge. Clearly this sabulously kinetic program is very useful to impress your enemies, and if you are paid by the word, to make you freakishly pronmial rich. Further, it could provide some relief from the xerophilus articles on politics or discussions of surreptitiously obscurius issues. And it will keep the spell-checkers busy, not to say baffled.

But, come to think of it, maybe we are both better off if I keep this secret to myself—or what would our writings come to?

COMMENCEMENT ADDRESS
(Unknown)

This appeared on the Internet as Kurt Vonnegut's commencement address at MIT. He claims he never wrote it, and, indeed, it appears that he never gave a commencement address at MIT. So this is a hoax. But it is such a good one and we enjoyed it so much (certainly a rarity in commencement speeches) that we thought to reproduce it. We don't know who wrote it, nor whether anyone has a copyright on it and if we are doing something illegal, please let us know. But at the moment, enjoy.

Ladies and gentlemen of the class of '97:

Wear sunscreen. If I could offer you only one tip for the future, sunscreen would be it. The long-term benefits of sunscreen have been proved by scientists, whereas the rest of my advice has no basis more reliable than my own meandering experience. I will dispense this advice now. Enjoy the power and beauty of your youth. Oh, never mind. You will not understand the power and beauty of your youth until they've faded. But trust me, in 20 years, you'll look back at photos of yourself and recall in a way you can't grasp now, how much possibility lay before you and how fabulous you really looked. You are not as fat as you imagine.

Don't worry about the future. Or worry, but know that worrying is as effective as trying to solve an algebra equation by chewing bubble gum. The real troubles in your life are apt to be things that never crossed your worried mind, the kind that blindside you at 4 P. M. on some idle Tuesday.

Do one thing every day that scares you.

Sing.

Don't be reckless with other people's hearts. Don't put up with people who are reckless with yours.

Floss.

Don't waste your time on jealousy. Sometimes you're ahead, sometimes you're behind. The race is long and, in the end, it's only with yourself.

Remember compliments you receive. Forget the insults. If you succeed in doing this, tell me how.

Keep your old love letters. Throw away your old bank statements.

Stretch.

Don't feel guilty if you don't know what you want to do with your life. The most interesting people I know didn't know at 22 what they wanted to do with their lives. Some of the most interesting 40-year-olds I know still don't.

Get plenty of calcium.

Be kind to your knees. You'll miss them when they're gone.

Maybe you'll marry, maybe you won't. Maybe you'll have children, maybe you won't. Maybe you'll divorce at 40,maybe you'll dance the funky chicken on your 75th wedding anniversary. Whatever you do, don't congratulate yourself too much, or berate yourself either. Your choices are half chance. So are everybody else's.

Enjoy your body. Use it every way you can. Don't be afraid of it or of what other people think of it. It's the greatest instrument you'll ever own.

Dance, even if you have nowhere to do it but your living room.

Read the directions, even if you don't follow them. Do not read beauty magazines. They will only make you feel ugly.

Get to know your parents. You never know when they'll be gone for good. Be nice to your siblings. They're your best link to your past and the people most likely to stick with you in the future.

Understand that friends come and go, but with a precious few, you should hold on. Work hard to bridge the gaps in geography and lifestyle, because the older you get, the more you need the people who knew you when you were young.

Live in New York City once, but leave before it makes you hard. Live in Northern California once, but leave before it makes you soft.

Travel.

Accept certain inalienable truths: Prices will rise. Politicians will philander. You, too, will get old. And when you do, you'll fantasize that when you were young, prices were reasonable, politicians were noble, and children respected their elders.

Respect your elders. Don't expect anyone else to support you. Maybe you have a trust fund. Maybe you'll have a wealthy spouse. But you never know when either one might run out.

Don't mess too much with your hair or by the time you're 40 it will look 85.

Be careful whose advice you buy, but be patient with those who supply it. Advice is a form of nostalgia. Dispensing it is a way of fishing the past from the disposal, wiping it off, painting over the ugly parts and recycling it for more than it's worth.

But trust me on the sunscreen.

Section Three
WHICH REMINDS ME

AN INTRODUCTION TO "WHICH REMINDS ME"

There is an old adage which says "If youth but knew what age could tell". This idea is much favored among the elderly as being an excuse to expound upon what (if anything) that we may have learned from life. We find and we think that this is common among our contemporaries, that we can remember a great deal of the adventures of the past but that we cannot recall them when we want to. Sometimes spontaneously for no reason and with no connection or at least no discernable connection with what is going on at the time. All of a sudden we remember something, sometimes of interest. We have lived reasonably adventurous lives and there are certain stories that we might tell which could be interesting. These are recorded not to teach any great moral truth or to persuade anyone to embrace some conviction but simply because we find them interesting. We hope you will too. We decided to put them down in as random a fashion as they occur to us. There is not necessarily any connection between one or the other nor are they really related. Here are things we remember. We will start each of them by saying "Which reminds me" without specifying what it was that reminded me for we frequently don't know.

We also introduce a certain element of chaos. Each remembrance starts immediately after the other, even if it may be at the bottom of the page. You will, we hope, get used to it.

ACCENT

(W. Umbreit)

Which reminds me that when I was still in graduate school at the University of Wisconsin, I was invited to give a lecture to the New York Academy of Sciences on some work I had published. This was a big event for me, one of the few times I had gotten out of the Midwest, and I even splurged on having an upper berth on the overnight train so that

I would not be too groggy. When I gave my lecture, I sensed that these people were too sophisticated to pay much attention to me, except for one man in the front row. So I gave my lecture to him. Afterwards he came up to me and after the usual, and usually insincere, comments he said "I pride myself on being able to locate where people come from by their accent. But yours puzzled me. What central European country did you come from? "

BAGGAGE AT ISTANBUL
(W. Umbreit)

Which reminds me that my wife and I were leaving Istanbul on an early flight to Beirut. These were the days in which all baggage was weighed. It was a rainy morning and when the cab delivered us to the airport, two porters took our baggage to the ticket counter. I got into a mild conversation with them, English mixed with low German suffices in most places and we talked about how miserable a morning it was and speculated as to whether the plane would be able to take off. When the baggage was all piled on to the scale, it was a little overweight, by maybe 10 pounds. The porter took off a small bag so that the weight of the remaining baggage was under the limit. The ticket clerk was busy and paid no attention to the process of weighing the baggage, then asked the porter if the baggage had been weighed. The porter said (truthfully), it had been weighed but did not mention that not all the baggage was on the scale at the moment. The clerk looked at the scale which containing the remaining baggage and since this weighed below the limits, he passes it on. The porter took the baggage from the scale, plus the handbag that he had removed and loaded them all onto the plane. When I was going to tip him, he shrugged me off with the implication that I could tip him later.

Shortly thereafter, the door from the outside burst open and an irate lady entered arguing with the taxi driver over the fare she had been charged. It was raining and early in the morning and a little extra surcharge was to be expected, but she did not see it that way. The airport porters witnessed this, of course, but they dutifully gathered her extensive luggage and put it on the scale. It was a little overweight, about as much as our luggage had been. But she began to berate the ticket clerk for the poor service she had been getting, and the exorbitant charges she had to pay for overweight, one of the porters looked at me, winked, and added two other bags, which had been sitting behind the counter, to the scale. It was now grossly overweight, and the ticket agent began to add up the extra charges, making the lady more and more agitated. However, that was what the scale showed and that is what she had to pay. It sometimes pays to be friendly and understanding with the people who serve you.

TRASH MAIL

(J. Wicks)

People, I observe, are wasteful. They may have some other traits which balance good with bad, but for now the subject of waste is urgent and worth considering. Where I live, one small room contains many, too many, mailboxes. I would not be so positive about that if I had not just been jostled by impatient people in a hurry to claim the latest delivery of mail left by our mailman. Also, there are two shiny metal hollow cylinders about three feet high in that small room, for deposit of empty envelopes and scrap paper items.

On some days the U. S. Postal Service delivers only letters from family members who could use a little extra money, and from business establishments which offer a choice of several amounts of money which we can and should send to them immediately.

But on practically all other days, our mailboxes contain advertisements and invitations to avail ourselves of some pretty attractive deals in plastic storm windows, plastic credit cards or even debit cards, automobile repairs, dry basement treatment, clothing, deeply discounted computers, investment advice and special promotional prices on almost everything sold by the grocery- produce - hardware supermarket and by drug stores. Here is where the waste begins.

Whole handfuls of this direct-mail advertising are stuffed into the cylindrical trash containers without even so much as a casual glance. Right now, I suppose, forests of maple and oaks and pines and whatever else they cut down for making paper, are being reduced to square miles of tree stumps, all to supply raw material for tons of paper used for all these advertising campaigns. So what do we do with the ads? We waste the whole thing. Not just the paper, which would be bad enough, but we waste all the creative writing activity which has taken place in advertising agencies, all the fancy color printing, and who knows how much concentrated effort in every Post Office, in all mail delivery trucks, airplanes, push carts, all in order to rush this material to us potential customers.

Now that you are feeling guilty and alarmed about the sheer waste of so much material and talent and effort, naturally you want to know how to correct this serious problem. First of all, you must take all the material you receive by mail to some quiet place and read every bit of it, carefully and receptively. Consider whether life might be much more interesting if you ordered at least some of the products and services offered. Read with understanding and acceptance every advertising circular, every invitation to subscribe, and take all the advertising material home with you for future reference.

There are very practical reasons for taking this mail seriously. We are told by economists and financial experts that we are living in a consumer-driven economy. Most of the money we spend goes through some complicated and possibly questionable business procedures which keep people working, paying taxes, supporting the life style we may or may not fully appreciate. Anyway, it is up to all of you to evaluate every advertised bargain and opportunity described in the direct mail delivered to us, and to buy or to subscribe or to contribute as much as you can, in order to keep our national economy healthy or at least alive.

Of course I might not have given this subject quite as much constructive thought except for the fact that the cylindrical trash containers were full to overflowing today when I tried to stuff all my own unread advertising junk mail into one of them.

CITIZEN OF ZURICH
(W. Umbreit)

Which reminds me that I am an honorary citizen of Zurich, Switzerland. This came about in the following fashion. I was spending a few days in Zurich waiting for a particular airplane to take back to the States. There is a river that runs through the center of Zurich the name of which I have forgotten but along its banks are several outdoor cafes where I used to eat lunch. One bright August day, I was having lunch. Two middle-aged gentlemen came out of the building across square from where I was sitting, and because the restaurant was crowded, I invited them to join me at my table. Which they did. However, they only spoke "Schweitzer Deutsche", which is a kind of German understandable only by the Swiss. My 'Hoch Deutsche' is not too good and has a Thuringian accent (not exactly low German but not entirely respectable either). And surely being Swiss, they must have known English or French. Maybe I just could not penetrate the accent. But they chose to speak their language, so our conversation was somewhat limited but we were getting along well. While we were sitting there having lunch, a group of pigeons settled in the trees above us, to which we paid no attention. But after a time the birds were frightened by some disturbance and they deposited materials, as is their custom, when they take flight. One of these deposits hit me on the shoulder and caused a bright white to gray band down the side of my somewhat dark jacket. While this was rather funny if somewhat embarrassing, these gentlemen thought it was absolutely hilarious. But as they were laughing, one could see some concern developing. Something was bothering them. Here was a stranger, evidently a tourist, who comes to their fair city, is shat on by a pigeon, and they laughed at him. So their attitude suddenly changed. They start to help me clean up. They sent for another order of food (which had also been showered by similar material) and one of them immediately went across the square into the building that they had emerged from half-hour earlier. He came back with a document and a small medallion and thereupon made me an "honorary citizen" of Zurich. The document with an elaborate red sealing wax seal (which I have to this day) was filled in with my name after he indicated that he had to have it spelled correctly. The document was then signed in my presence. They then gave me the small medallion as evidence that I was now an honorary citizen. It turned out that I had been having lunch with the mayor and his secretary of the city of Zurich and am now an "honorary citizen" of that remarkable metropolis and am entitled to the privileges thereof and beholden to the duties required, if I could only find out what they are.

CAMEL SADDLE
(W. Umbreit)

Which reminds me, my wife and I were driving down beyond Bersheba at the edge of the Negev dessert in Israel close to what is today the Gaza strip. This is near the southern end of biblical Israel which extended from Dan (in the north) to Bersheba (in the south). While traveling we came across a native flea market. There were a variety of people there selling all sorts of things, but one, a rather handsome Bedouin, made a serious effort to sell my wife a camel saddle.

Doris Umbreit

When she protested that she did not have a camel, and did not know how to ride one, he pointed out that with a little work and much polish, this particular camel saddle would make an excellent trinket to have in the living room and would certainly be unique and an excellent conversation piece, and that if we bought it he would take us on a ride on his camel so that we could say that we had ridden a camel with this very saddle. The Bedouin, of course, lived in the desert. So far as I could tell, he did not have contacts outside of the Negev nor had he been to any western type school or university. He spoke a mixture of English. French, and Arabic, but well enough so that we could make out what he was saying. And here he was devising an intelligent and semi-convincing scenario designed to sell the saddle. Indeed, if we were not limited by the baggage that we could carry on the subsequent plane, we might have been convinced. A very smart fellow from a very primitive society.

PLEASURES OF WRITING

(J. Wicks)

I am lacking something. And I do not miss it or care. Games, amusements, entertainment, I find most of them boring, so I avoid them. To a certain degree, that means that I also tend to neglect the friendly contact with some fine people whom I like. The problem is that their enjoyment of the activities that I find so tiresome leaves us very little to share. There are a few exceptions, and I will comment on them a little later. But for now, when I grow weary after too-long intervals of reading or desk work, I occasionally enjoy writing whatever recollections may come to mind.

There is a quiet pleasure in recording some thoughts which will probably never be read. There is no need to seek the approval or appreciation of some strangers I have never met, no requirement to write for any other purpose than my own selfish relaxation. It is nice if what one has written is available to others, friends, children, grandchildren and passing critics. Today we can do just this with the computer. I can write what I like and put it on a disk and give it to my children and to those who I think might like it. And there it is, for them to read as a book, or to print out and have a book.

BURMA SHAVE

(W. Umbreit)

Which reminds me that in the early 1930's, there used to be along the highways an occasional set of signs advertising a shaving cream (I gather one of the earliest types) called Burma Shave. I remember these vividly and found many to be very amusing. They looked something like the sign below.

They were eventually discontinued because auto speeds increased and they became a distracting attention diversion and the cost of maintenance increased tremendously.

IN THIS VALE

OF TOIL AND SIN

THE HEAD GROWS BALD

BUT NOT THE CHIN

BURMA SHAVE

REDUNDANCY

(J. Wicks)

> I really don't know what to call this.
> It's not about words.
> It's not about meaning.
> It's not about writing.
> For heavens sake, what is it about?

But that's the point. Instead of saying what this essay is about, I said what it was not about. And I took three sentences to say this, ending up with nothing. This is the problem I want to talk about. What is the word? Redundancy. We spend so much time and effort avoiding the point, that we sometimes miss it altogether.

Listen to almost any political speech today. It is not this, it is not that, it is only about vote for me. Watching television news, for example, one finds the same scenes, words, and comments, over and over again, identical, they came from replaying the same tape. That is what our contact with the world has become, a replaying of tape.

One may argue, of course, that the constant repetition of "it is not" this or that, is done for emphasis, but clearly such an approach wastes a lot of time, space, and even attention. We soon tune out; our attention wanders.

But notice something. I've used "re-play tape" and "tune out", terms not in use 20 years ago. Indeed the electronic age has overwhelmed us. The average household, indeed the average desktop, is filled with electronic gadgets whose purpose is to repeat, and repeat, and repeat assigned tasks. Of course, the television screen is a continual renewal of line after line of dots, or pixels, or whatever they are called. And the computer, marvelous as is it, is a continual mini-second scanning of electronic charges.

We live in a world of redundancy—the same things over and over again. We use a thousand electronic flashes to convey the word "word" and a million more to sustain the picture on a television screen. What a waste of flashes. What redundancy.

BUREAU DRAWER

(W. Umbreit)

PRAVDA IS HONEST?

Which reminds me that once, when I was in Moscow, Pravda (the main Russian Newspaper, English Edition) published a short article which said in effect, "Here we are, the USSR is the greatest nation on earth, we are the only people who have a medallion on the moon. So why is it that we cannot build a bureau drawer that fits?"

Which also reminds me that one day Pravda came out with a front page article, including photographs, showing the police beating up the students in New York who were conducting a peaceful demonstration. When I got back home and looked it up, Pravda was almost right. There were cops beating up students, who were trying to disrupt the peaceful demonstration known as the commencement ceremony at Columbia University.

Which also reminds me of the day that the students took over the main building of Columbia University. I was there in the main building in a conference room together with a committee considering a research grant applied for by some scientists at Columbia. I don't remember what the grant was about, or who wanted it, or whether we decided to give it to them or not. What I do remember is that the door to the hallway was blocked. The entire area was filled with shouting students. So, in order to get out, we had to climb out on a windowsill and jump down about 4 feet. Thank goodness that the conference room was on the first floor.

ATHLETES ARE TOUGH
(W. Umbreit)

I see among my contemporaries living in this retirement community, many who were once very athletic: who swam (or does one say 'swum'?), or played golf, or skated, or played tennis, or what not. They are mostly vigorous people, whose athletic experiences very probably made them healthier than they would otherwise have been at their age. But I notice two things. One is they complain vigorously about how their performance was not as good as it was a year or two ago. This is very disappointing because they feel that they are at the peak of their skills, and further practice can only improve their performance. Further their opponents, in competitive games, are also slowing down, but not as fast as they, so the whole game becomes something of a disappointment. Further, their opponents are becoming more crabby and less tolerant of those little accidents and omissions that are bound to occur to everybody.

The other thing I notice is that as far as the game is concerned, they have no sense whatsoever. They go out in the blazing sun (without sunscreen—never used it! and I hate to wear a hat!) at 90 degrees and bake themselves thoroughly. They come back exhausted and complain about how bad things were, and how they could not get into "top form". But they never seem to realize that their bodies are no longer able to withstand the 'slings and arrows', the stress that earlier they ignored. Indeed, they have probably done themselves more harm than they have gained by their athletic activity.

And here I see something else, which is quite serious. These people have been associated with their athletic activity for many years and are still absorbed in it. But in a relatively short time, if they keep up this behavior, they will no longer be able to play it, even by reduced standards. Their knees and shoulders will hurt, their back can no longer take it, etc. So what to do? You have to give up the game or activity such as the exercise and the excitement of winning, the feeling of contentment of a job well done. But do you have anything to replace it? Any less vigorous activity which your strength permits, which can occupy your time? This is the important point, because this is the time that one must develop just such different interest which will occupy one's time and give one a focus, something you are interested in doing, something that can give your life meaning, or at least keep you busy with minor problems associated with your new activity.

If you can no longer engage in your favorite athletic activity, all is not lost. You have something else to occupy you. After seeing some of my friends, exhausted from a nine hole round of golf, I try to suggest something less rigorous. They tell me they played golf (or tennis, or what not) three times a week since they retired, and which they always will do, Monday, Wednesday, and Friday afternoon, rain or shine, because they have a reserved place at the golf club and there they meet their friends. This is their whole life. What else should they do? A little rest will cure them. And it generally does. But will it a few months from now? And in the meantime they ought to cut back a little and find something else, less stressful but productive of satisfaction, at least to them? Several suggestions come to mind. They could knit, maybe a new pair of socks, or a shawl for their grandmother. Or they could carve wood, or learn to play the flute (neighbors permitting), or even open a computer. In the latter case it is helpful to have a grandson to get one over the rough spots since computers seem to have a mind of their own and do not always obey perfectly straightforward requests. Or one could learn (if one did not already know) how to play bridge, or solitaire, or scrabble or other games of the intellect. It is more rewarding than playing the stock market, but that could be done too, if one has an even temper and plenty of capital. One could take up short wave radio, or the piano, or try exotic cooking (I would not recommend exotic dancing, too vigorous) or any of a number of reasonable but more sedentary activities. But the aging athlete really needs to find something else to do, and should find some less strenuous activity. Of course they should. But will they?

And I expound upon this theme. In spite of the fact that my popularity has taken a decided downward trend. But I am persistent! I would make a good preacher, if I had the energy. My new activity to replace my minor athletic interests, is to reform the world. It really needs it. But do they listen?

Of course not. Who would give up a fine game of golf just because it is killing you?

SOME THOUGHTS ON CRITICISM

(J. Wicks)

Professional reviewers of books, plays, motion pictures, television programs etc., all serve some useful purpose, I suppose. But too often they leave me with a feeling that they are trying to convey the impression that they know much more than the creators of the material or performance under review. And they, the reviewers, could have done far better than the authors or directors or performers about whom they are writing reviews.

Years ago there was an appearance which, so far as I know, was never recorded in the area of criticism or review. It was advertised sparingly as "Charles Laughton--Readings". During his long and rather flamboyant career, Laughton was the subject, and often the object of reviews ranging from "gross over-acting", "tasteless" all the way to "powerful performance", "deeply moving". Perhaps there were some elements of truth in each extreme criticism, but too often I thought that the critics own vanity showed through his or her review.

One evening I recall now, the stage of the auditorium was furnished with only two articles: a rather high stool with a seat that seemed obviously inadequate and a small mahogany table. At the exact time advertised, Laughton walked on-stage, carrying an armful of books, which he placed on the table. Then he looked at the audience with what appeared to be rather petulant disapproval, or possibly some indigestion.

He never touched any of the books again. He cautiously lowered his substantial weight on the seat of the high stool. For forty-five minutes he shared with the audience his favorite excerpts from his life-long fascination with good reading. He included a wide spectrum of authors and subjects and style, all spoken in an apparently effortless conversational manner. The contrast with the florid intensity of most of his roles was almost startling. He appeared to be calmly enjoying a friendly discussion of ideas and material which had provided him with food for thought during his obvious hectic life. And he was wearing his learning lightly. Obviously not the stuff professional reviewers delight in critically analyzing with condescension.

It was a demonstration, among other matters, of a remarkably disciplined memory. I never saw a review of the performance in the next day's newspapers.

GET LOST

(W. Umbreit)

Which reminds me that I was in Stockholm, and had a few days off, so I went to Oslo over in Norway, which I found difficult to live in. The Norwegians would seem to come into a restaurant acting perfectly normal, but after a few drinks they would get into terrible rows. After barely escaping such a row in a hotel restaurant, I pulled out of Oslo and went to Berlin. I left Oslo at 8 am and at noon I was on a bus in East Berlin. After a day or so in Berlin I got restless and went to Munich, then by train <u>via</u> Lake Constance to Zurich and then to Paris. Clearly I was a little restless. I was sitting in a café on the left bank, looking across at Notre Dame, when a thought occurred to me. I could get lost. No one knew where I was. It would take them days before they could trace me. And in the meantime, I had enough travelers checks on me so that I could live for perhaps a month. I could cash them all at one spot and that would be the last anyone would hear of me. I could really get lost. But where would I go? One spot would be the Loire Valley southwest of Tours, France. But I would probably find it hard to get a job there and I would need a way to get false papers, documents etc. That made me think of Switzerland, where I had heard there was such a business, but I didn't know how to make contact. Still if I were to go to Switzerland, I would go to Lugano. This was near Italy and had a mixed Swiss-Italian flavor, not as rigid as the German parts of Switzerland. It was nicely located, less than 30 minutes by air from the main centers of Europe such as Paris, Rome, Berlin, Vienna. Living was relatively inexpensive and I could probably get a job, dishwashing maybe. Yes, an ideal spot.

I was somewhat shocked at such a thought but there it was. But I probably lacked courage. And the problems were somewhat greater than I had first thought. It would get me involved with the criminal element in Europe and I had no experience in this area. So I decided not to abandon my present way of life, hectic though it might be, because it had many rewards and satisfactions and that getting lost was not the way to face one's problems. So that relaxed me and I took the next plane home.

FAMILY ROOTS
(W. Umbreit)

Which reminds me, my family came from a little town called Wolfis, in Thuringia, just over the border from Bavaria in East Germany. I never got to see the place, but as East Germany opened up, other members of my family have seen it. The church records only go back to after the Thirty Years War, the church having been burned down at that time. But it is possible to trace our ancestry (with some gaps) back to that time.

I had an uncle, who specialized on oriental languages, was a missionary to Japan for many years and then went to Berlin to edit a German newspaper for his church, by which time he had become a bishop. He was interested in genealogy and found a certain Peter (I think) Umbreit who was the castillian of a famous castle close by, the Ehrfurth castle. He wrote to the Duke of Saxe-Gotha in whose area the castle exists, inquiring about Peter and got a reply from the Duke's secretary which said that yes, there was such a man and yes, he was the castillian of the castle for the proper period and then the letter added "Since he occupied such a high position, it is unlikely that he was a relative of yours".

I was giving a lecture at a provincial university in Puerto Rico (Mayaguez) when I was stopped in the hallway by a man who asked me if I was W. Umbreit. When I said yes, he said "So am I" and gave me his card showing him to be Werner Umbreit, radio engineer. I said that with a name like that he must be a relative and since he seems to be clearly German, I said that we came from Thuringia. He said, Oh no, his family came from Wofis and it took me some time to convince him that this town was in Thuringia. He later visited me in the US and became the radio engineer for several radio stations in Frankfurt (most of these broadcast in English since there were large contingents of US troops near Frankfurt).

I was later taken to Mayaguez by a professor from the University of Puerto Rico. He took me (and his daughter who was returning to college) to breakfast, and after he paid the bill he received a large fistful of bills in exchange. I remarked on this, and he said that he had paid the waiter with a $100 bill. I said I had never seen one, so he opened his wallet and showed me one. He said that he had been gambling the night before at the Casinos in San Juan and had won $200.

When his daughter had been delivered to her dormitory, he said that his wife did not like him to gamble so he could not tell his daughter, but that he had had a few drinks and had bet more than he should have but that he had won $2000, out of which he proposed that we should spend the week-end celebrating. Which is probably why I can't remember much more.

SOME THOUGHTS ON SILENCE

(J. Wicks)

It is difficult to determine whether we have surrendered, or been robbed, of one of civilized mankind's most valuable treasures. All we can know with certainty is that is it gone. The enjoyment of frequent soothing intervals of quiet can never again be ours, even in the unlikely possibility that we might rediscover its value. The capacity of enjoying silent intervals is linked in some definite way to the process of thinking, or, more accurately expressed, to the function of creative thinking. As we lose the delights of quiet interludes, we tend to abandon ability, and worse yet desire, to think any original thoughts.

Noise pollution can be traced to many sources, most of which are either individual in nature or collective. Much of today's mindless, unceasing babble that is incorrectly called conversation is the most insidious form of individual destruction of silence. Too many people consider their own monologue recital of unimportant and uninteresting details to be their inalienable right. The incessant talker accomplishes two objectives: he, or she, suspends all constructive thinking while talking, and at the same time prevents anyone within hearing distance from concentration. He is not an entertainer as he wants to be. He is simply a large bore. Groups of three or more compulsive talkers squeeze out of existence all shreds of quiet moments. Also, a collective inescapable destruction of quiet surrounds us now wherever we may go. Every store, every shopping mall, even banks and offices must provide recorded musical trash in an endless stream, to guard against the possibility that there might be some moments of silence. In many office buildings, even the brief interval of riding up or down in elevators is invaded by recorded tune from a master control in the bowels of the building. Physicians' waiting rooms, nursing homes, dentist offices all joining in the conspiracy of multiple musical mediocrity for the purpose of preventing peaceful stillness.

Silence itself is not merely the absence of sound. It is an environment.

Silence can be healing, comforting, even a soothing therapy for weary sufferers. But it can also provide opportunities for creative thought in minds which are capable of concentration. Long before Beethoven wrote his last, magnificent, ninth symphony he was plunged into a life of silence by tragic deafness. Generations of musically cultured audiences have been inspired by the sheer beauty of the Finale, based on Schiller's "Ode to Joy". It was composed in total silence. Ludwig van Beethoven never heard his Ninth Symphony. But you and I never would have heard it either, if his creative hours had been sabotaged by piped-in musical trash.

It is unlikely that there will ever be an end to excessive witless small talk, or to the relentless outpouring of tasteless musical trivia in almost all public places. We have to wonder what, if anything, can be done to escape, even temporarily, to the restoring therapy of occasional silence. Any people who have enough intelligence to recognize today's deadly destruction of quiet can develop an intellectual discipline for self-help. Short intervals of time can be set aside to withdraw from all sounds of noise pollution, for the purpose of consciously relishing the peace of undefiled quiet moments. And who knows? Perhaps an increasing awareness and appreciation of the creative potential of deliberately selected times of stillness may develop into one of the most rewarding of experiences: the sheer luxury of original thinking.

But first we must learn to appreciate occasional refreshing silence.

DAVIDIANS
(W.Umbreit)

Which reminds me that my wife and I, together with a friend who lived in Israel together with his wife, were driving down from the Dead Sea to Elot, on the gulf of Akaba where they were going to spend Yom Kippur. All of a sudden, my friend turned off the highway onto a small side road. His wife protested, where was he going? He said that there was an American who had established a small colony here, devoted to life as it was in the time of King David. He had several wives and many children and there was a colony of about 25 people altogether. He thought they might be interesting.

After driving about two miles we came to a camp surrounded by barbed wire and there were two watch towers. At the gate to this camp there was a small shed, stacked from floor to ceiling with cases of coke and other soft drinks (not cooled) and presided over by a rather large and fat young man. We asked why he had his soda stand so far from the highway and he said that this way it was less trouble. He said he was from Waco, Texas, and was the day guard for the camp. The founder of the camp and most of the men were off working in a factory. The guard let us in to freely wander about and we talked to several of the wives. They seemed to take the situation of multiple wives as normal, although I do not recall that David had more than one wife at a time.

It was hot and miserable and we did not stay too long. On the way back we passed the factory. We asked about the watch towers and they said that they were sometimes attacked at night by Bedouins (they thought) or by Arabs from Jordan (only about two miles to the east). We left and thought very little more about them, until the shootout in Waco, Texas, at the colony of the Branch Davidians and I would be willing to bet that the people we saw that day in the desert were probably those involved at Waco. It is strange indeed to reflect upon one's encounters which seem to have no significance at the time, yet prove to be of great interest later.

IMPOSSIBLE COINCIDENCE

(W. Umbreit)

Which reminds me that once, when I was in Aberdeen in August, there was a heat wave and the temperature reached 60 F. The city of Aberdeen closed down- it was too hot to work. With summer clothing I was reasonably comfortable— but the Scots all wore woolens and were sweltering. While there, I visited the Rowett Institute, a research laboratory just outside of Aberdeen, which, in those days, was populated mostly by brilliant men who did not get along with the establishment at Cambridge, Oxford, or London. Rowett was also famous for its 'Scotch Cellar' which contained samples of all the different types of single malt scotch made in the British Isles. Not only were they kept there, they could be sampled and compared. Rowett later became famous for its animal cloning experiments and "Dolly", the cloned sheep, had her picture in every newspaper in the world.

On an entirely different subject, a young lady graduate student at Cornell whose name I have forgotten, but who I will call Miss Gretchen to emphasize her German origins, contacted me because she was having trouble measuring the respiration of turkey sperm in the "Warburg" apparatus, on which I had written a book. I always wondered how these people ever collected samples of turkey sperm, and if they told me, I have forgotten. I soon found the trouble. The usual method of cleaning the reaction flasks was to put them, after washing, in "cleaning solution" which consisted of potassium dichromate in concentrated sulfuric acid, guaranteed to remove all traces of organic matter. As the flasks became slight etched, due to continued use, the glass tended to retain some chromium ions, and while this was tolerable in bacteria and in animal tissue slices, it greatly inhibited the respiration of ground up tissue or, in this case, sperm. So one had to clean the flasks used in tissue preparations by boiling them in concentrated nitric acid, a procedure that nobody liked.

Some time later, I was attending a symposium for "Jimmy" Sumner, a professor at Cornell, who was the first man to crystallize an enzyme (urease) and as he always said "the last man to get the credit for it". He was awarded the Nobel Prize for this achievement. When I was at Cornell, isolating the enzymes associated with Vitamin B6, I would go to see him frequently, because he had an uncanny feeling about how proteins would act and after I told him what I had done (which did not work) he would frequently make suggestions that would solve the problem.

At the banquet of the symposium I was seated between Major X (whose name I have also forgotten) and Miss Gretchen. Major X was the director, or assistant director, of the Rowett Insitute. In the course of the conversation, Major X said that he had been in the British Royal Air Force and had been involved in the raid on Permunde. At which point Miss Gretchen let out a shriek and fainted. Now Permunde was a base in Northwest Germany from which the v-bombs were launched against London and it had been damaged by an attack of 450 bombers. Next to it was a concentration camp in which the 10 year old Miss Gretchen had been confined and she had been wounded and severely frightened by the raid. She had done her best to try to forget the incident, but its sudden revelation was too much for her. This always seemed to me to be one of those impossible coincidences which do occur, in spite of the laws of chance and the dispersion of people

THANKSGIVING DAY 1970

(J. Wicks)

(En Route from Beirut to Istanbul) Which reminds me that Thanksgiving Day is resting in the sunshine in Beirut, Lebanon, learning how blue the sea can be. It is seeing cedars of Lebanon and palm trees growing. And abrupt mountains towering almost the edge of the beaches. It is hearing Lebanese and French and English, and, as everywhere, German, spoken by people who look surprisingly the same as any group stepping out of the subway at 42nd street in New York. It is watching a huge bearded Sikh adjusting his turban. It is catching the eye of a tiny Japanese child and exchanging smiles.

Thanksgiving is feeling grateful for being alive, only minutes after the captain of the plane has announced to his passengers, "We are having a problem with our left landing gear. Ladies and gentleman do not be alarmed."

It isn't really Thanksgiving just because people at home are having family dinners and watching football games and resting from work, until you feel compelled to breathe the silent prayer, "Thank God, Thank God".

HISTORY FABLES
(W. Umbreit)

Which reminds me, don't you ever wonder about what you are taught in History? Is it true? Or more likely, some writer's idea as to what it must have been like. Take Ancient Egypt for example. A very primitive culture, using slaves and cattle-drawn carts to build the pyramids. Of course, we couldn't build an Egyptian sized pyramid today, and that must be because our slaves are not muscular;

they sit in cubicles and work computers. But if we can read hieroglyphs, which are mostly about the gods and how great the pharaohs were, we should be able to find some that tell us what life was really like. Of course, they fished and hunted duck (although with less expensive equipment than we use today; I have heard that the rifle, camouflage shelter, and decoys, and upkeep of dogs runs to $5,000-just to fool a duck). But they could not be really civilized since they did not have golf.

Well maybe this idea is wrong. Below is a picture from one of the tombs in the upper cliffs of the Valley of the Kings. I'm not sure that it is from the tomb of Reckmeyer (a somewhat Jewish name for an Egyptian) who was a scribe who made pots full of money and who wrote a long poem about being a scribe. Don't be a peasant, he said, and have to pay taxes. Be a scribe and steal what you want. But it could be that history is misleading?

(from Keller "The Bible As history"
(1956).

Look at this picture. These people are loading a television set (at arrow) and the little fellow just behind the right donkey is carrying a golf club. The two golfers on the golf-cart (donkey) are supplied with a quantity of Egyptian beer, known to be the best in the world. And you tell me they weren't civilized.

TAXES IN THE SOVIET UNION

(W.Umbreit)

Which reminds me that I was once in a bar in Moscow and fell into a conversation with member of the science academy. We compared the systems in the US and the USSR. Of course, their taxes are very low, and so are their wages.

That is, everything is taken out before they get any money. I tried to make the point that we got the money and then paid it back in taxes and said that in Britain and the US the income tax was of the order of 30-35%. The man responded by saying that this was purely Russian propaganda. One should not believe this. Why if taxes were that high nobody would be able to live.

STREPTOMYCIN PRODUCTION
(W. Umbreit)

Which reminds me that I was in Prague attending a symposium on antibiotics. We were taken to an antibiotic production facility outside of the city. This consisted of a series of one to two story buildings (with one four story). We were taken to a small two story building in which they were producing penicillin. The system was rather crude-they had about three 250 gallon tanks clearly transferred from a brewery. They were producing penicillin but I could also smell streptomycin. I questioned them and they said, I guess truthfully, that in this building they only produced penicillin. So finally I caught on and asked if they produced streptomycin in any other building. After some consultation they said yes so I asked to be taken there. With some reluctance they took me to the four story building in which was located a magnificent, very modern plant for streptomycin production equal to, and possibly even surpassing, most such plants in the US. Their piping was all glass and one could see the fluid running through it so if any clogs occurred they could immediately be located. A truly magnificent plant of which they could be proud. What has always puzzled me is why they were so reluctant to show it to us especially since we were presumably familiar with the production facilities elsewhere and especially since they had such fine facilities to show. Why did they not want us to know that they had facilities which possibly surpassed ours?

HOTEL ST ANNE

(W. Umbreit)

Which reminds me that I was attending a biochemical congress in Paris and I had taken my wife along. We were housed in the University dormitories which she did not like because the men's and women's toilet facilities were both in one large room and the women had to go through the men's facilities before getting to theirs. So she went over the right bank and found a hotel, the Hotel St Anne. It is close to the opera but is really a hotel for French traveling men and only the concierge spoke English but he was very helpful. They had an open elevator right in the center of the lobby which went up four stories, the elevator that is. While everything in the hotel was French, there was, in the elevator, a little notice, carved in Ivory, which said in English, "If there is an anomaly in the operation of this elevator, please call the porter".

There was a difficulty with the hotel, however. One could not get a Paris taxi driver to take you there. I never did learn how to pronounce French but the drivers would just stare at me when I gave them directions. Finally I got the concierge to write out that I wanted to go to the Hotel St Anne, and this worked. I found out that the street the hotel was on, and after which it was named, was once the site of a famous insane asylum –called 'the Hotel St Anne'-and the phrase "go to the hotel St Anne" meant in the slang of the street "you must be crazy".

AIRPORTS
(W. Umbreit)

Which reminds me that when I was in the Tokyo airport, I saw in the shop a bottle of Sake, the Japanese wine. I really don't like Sake, but this was made by the Toume Manufacturing Co. of Nagasaki Japan. I bought it because I now had a bottle of "Sake Toume". This could easily be pronounced "Sock It To Me".

Which reminds me, I was in the airport at Hong Kong waiting for a flight to Tokyo when I got into a conversation with an Englishman who had spend most of his life as a copra grower in Malaysia.

We discussed the price of copra, and how difficult times were for the plantation owners and he was ready to quit. He was going back to England for the first time in 40 years and while I tried to point out that it was not like the England he had left as a young man, I really made no impression. Our discussion was interrupted by a man from New York University, whom I knew only slightly, but who had been traveling in the boondocks of India, and was so glad to see someone who spoke American, that he just bubbled over-and talked non-stop until his plane was called. I quite understood his reaction having only recently gone through the same situation where I could finally find someone from home whom I could talk to. When he left, I turned to my planter friend with a shrug. He asked me where the man lived and I said New York. "My Gosh", he said, "that is a place that I would bloody well avoid".

Which reminds me of the Old Pan Am terminal at Kennedy in New York. It was a large curricular building whose sides were open to the air. Whoever designed and built it had never lived through a winter in New York. At any rate, I was waiting for a plane for London, and after that to go on to Moscow. I had planned to take my wife and my daughter, who was interested in Russian History, but at the last minute they were unable to go. At the flight desk I had been handed their passports (as well as mine) since they had had to be sent to the consulate of the USSR some weeks before. I didn't want to carry them with me, but I could not find an envelope to send them home. The few shops that were open did not have a single envelope. While I was stewing about this I saw a suitable envelope being pushed about by the breeze, so I ran and grabbed it. It was addressed to me! And it was the envelope that had contained the passports from the consulate. The shops had stamps so I was able to send the passports home.

DON'T DRIVE

(W. Umbreit)

There is a story going about our institution about four old gentlemen, like ourselves, who are complaining about the increasing difficulties of their lives. One says that he can no longer read— his eyes are so bad that he can hardly see anything. The second says that his Parkinson's is so bad that he can hardly hold a fork and his wife has to feed him so that the food gets into his mouth. The third says that he is getting Alzheimer's disease and he no longer knows which direction he is going nor can he remember where he was or what he was doing. The fourth says that they are taking too dim a view of life. Look on the bright side; YOU CAN STILL DRIVE.

In our little group, those who have given up driving find this amusing and all too true. Those who still insist on driving do not find it very funny, again because it is all too true. There are those whose bonds of affection with their car, or rather the freedom of movement and opportunity it gives them, will simply not be broken and they retain the car and the freedom it implies until the bitter end. And that is just what it can be-a very bitter end. There ought to be an effective way to prevent such marginal drivers from endangering themselves or others. But our laws and their enforcement are not very effective and many older people are driving who should not be.

But what I wish to say is that being without a car is not so difficult. I don't have to memorize how may feet a car takes to stop when traveling at 30, 35, 40, or even 60 miles an hour, heaven forbid that we should go so fast. That's for teenagers who are just learning to drive, whereas we know better. I don't have to take a driver's test. I don't have to pay car insurance and don't have to have a reserved parking space. I don't have expenses of car upkeep and oil changes and tire replacement. I am free of all those difficulties. Of course, I can't go anywhere.

Well, there is that, but it is not as bad as you might suppose. If I need groceries, my children and grandchildren can take me to the stores. That's much easier than riding the bus. The home in which I live has a bus that goes at scheduled times to various shopping centers. I can even hire a private driver to take me to the train station or the airport, and while this sounds expensive, it is much less than paying for car insurance (providing I go to the airport less than once a month). That is, with a little ingenuity I can manage to get my outside needs done, and I don't really enjoy shopping that much. So it is not so bad.

LENINGRAD WORKERS UNION
(W. Umbreit)

Which reminds me that I was a member (for a time) of the Leningrad Electromechanical Workers Union. It came about in this way. Our antibiotic delegation (4 members) were in Leningrad (now St Petersburg) and as recreation one Sunday we were taken by our KGB guides to Peterhof, the palace of Catherine and of Peter the Great not far outside of Leningrad. We got there early and as we passed an elegant restaurant (we could read enough Russian to know the "pectopah" meant restaurant). We realized that we were hungry. To the consternation of our KGB guides we insisted on going in, and since they could find no reasonable excuse as to why we should not have breakfast, in we went.

The dining room was partially filled with members of the Leningrad Electro-mechanical Workers Union and we were a subject of curiosity for them. To be friendly we bought them some wine (in the region a good red wine was frequently served with breakfast) and we became friends. They were putting on an entertainment and they invited us to join. One of our delegation decided not to stay, he had work in Leningrad and went back home, accompanied by one KGB man. The other was a jolly fellow and joined in the fun. We went to their performance and afterward they invited us to join them on a picnic on the lake. I have a fine photograph of me being rowed by a lady blacksmith on that lake. When it came time to leave, some of them wanted to ride in our limousine, presumably they had never ridden in one before, so we took them for a ride. They took us to their factory, and let us inside to see where they worked and, with the permission of the KGB man, who was also having a good time, they made us honorary members of the Leningrad Electromechanical Workers Union. Since I have never seen that this has been revoked, I may still be a (non-dues paying) member

POLIO VACCINE PRODUCTION IN KIEV

(W. Umbreit)

Which reminds me that as a member of the U.S. delegation on antibiotics visiting the Soviet Union, we were taken to a laboratory and production unit engaged in producing the 'Salk' (formaldehyde killed) vaccine although the Soviet Union publicly favored the 'live' vaccine. At any rate, we were shown some of the facilities. I suppose that we were shown the best parts (who would want these foreigners to see the worst?). The production was in tissue culture flasks, not greatly different from that in the U.S. but it was summer, and it was hot, so the windows were open. There were no screens on them so the laboratory and the production facilities were loaded with flies. We were impressed enough to get out of these facilities as soon as we could. We never found out whether they had illness in the area surrounding the facilities, but we would be surprised if some infection did not occur.

MILAN
(W. Umbreit)

Which reminds me of two incidents in Milan which have remained in my memory. As you know, the cathedral in Milan (the Duomo) has spires on each of its flying buttresses. As you may not know, it also has a fast food stand on its roof. I used to eat there frequently. It was faster and certainly much less expensive than to eat in the "galleries" below. One day, while having a late lunch, a workman came out on the roof dragging a 8 to 12 ft two by four ladder which has some cross bars nailed to it at about intervals of a foot. He dragged it to the end of the roof, swung it out over the space till it reached the bottom of the spire on the flying buttress, jumped over the intervening space and proceeded to set up the two by four ladder against the spire so he could get near the top to repair it. This he did. But I was so frightened at these antics that I could no longer eat and had to leave.

Which also reminds me that I was attending a scientific conference on Antibiotics and was chairman of a session on their mode of action. It was in September and was very hot, as Septembers in Northern Italy can be. The meeting hall was a narrow room, holding about 200 people, without air conditioning and it was full. A chairman usually just introduces the speakers but it was so hot in the hall that I had to do something, so I said that as Chairman I would make a ruling that if you took off your coat and hung it over the back of the chair, I would rule that this was equivalent to wearing it and that is what I was going to do and I hoped that someone would follow me. The Americans, the British, and the Canadians and some Scandinavians did so, but the majority, who were Italian, did not. At the end of the first presentation, I repeated this ruling and told the story of the Arab who rode his camel while his wife walked 20 paces behind, but since the war there were mines in the desert and now the Arab still rode his camel but his wife now walked 20 ft. in front, showing that age-old customs could be changed by necessity. This time the French took off their coats but I figured I had lost. Sitting in the front row was a dignified Italian gentleman, who I later learned was the highly respected Professor Califano. About halfway through the second paper, he got up, took off his coat, hung it over the chair. So did all the other Italians. Then we saw what the difficulty was. He was wearing suspenders, about two inches wide, on which were hand painted nudes. The Russians, the Poles and those from Eastern Europe, then under Soviet domination, never did take off their coats. Presumably they could not get permission from Moscow, where it was undoubtedly more comfortable.

RUG FROM KASHMIR

(W. Umbreit)

Which reminds me, I was in Srinigar in Kashmir and hired a taxi to take me up into the Himalayan mountains on the border of Tibet. There were no tours to this area at the time since there was a war between India and Pakistan and this area was sort of involved. On the way out of town, the driver stopped at a small hut, because, he said, he wanted to show me something (for which he got a commission, I am sure, such being the way of life here). What he showed me was a weaving room where a man and his six sons were hand weaving a rug. The oldest son was about 16, the youngest about six, and they all sat in a row pulling varied colored threads through a series of vertical threads (although somewhat larger than threads) attached to the loom. Their instructions for making the intricate pattern were attached to the loom by a thumbtack and the entire instruction was on a crumpled sheet of brown paper about 4 inches wide and maybe 5 inches deep. This was not, so far as I could judge, a tourist shop, it was too far out of the way to attract much tourist attention. I believed that it was a real production unit. The rug was about half finished, and I liked the design so after some negotiations (inevitable in this part of the world), I bought it. Then I said, "How do I know that you will send me this identical rug, and not some rug made by machine in Calcutta or Bombay?" He said, we will put a white string in it." So he had his youngest son insert a white thread at the edge of the rug just at the edge of the intricate design that he was weaving. You could see the white thread if you looked for it, but it was otherwise not noticeable.

Some months later the rug arrived in burlap wrap. I wanted the rug as a decoration, not as a rug, so I hung it on the wall and it moved with us as we moved from one residence to another. Over the course of time I had forgotten entirely about the thread until after moving to this retirement community I was showing some new acquaintances what a fine rug I had, when I suddenly remembered the white thread, and there it was—just as had been promised years earlier in a small hut in northern Kashmir.

SOLOMON'S MINES
(W. Umbreit)

Which reminds me that on the same trip that we visited the Davidians, my friend also stopped at an active copper mine. The hills on either side of the Rift Valley from the Dead Sea to the Gulf, are bright red in color with streaks of blue-green in them, indicative of copper. The copper mine was closely guarded and they did not accept visitors, but my friend was from the Israeli Research Institute in Rehovoth, and that carried some weight, so we were allowed in.

A rather young engineer was assigned to us and after showing us the process of mining and refining copper, he took us to the top of a slag heap where we could see far into the surrounding country. Well, he said, "I know what you want to ask me, which is "Is this Solomon's' mine?" That I can tell you, the answer is no. The ore we have here and from which you saw us extract the copper, is an ore that could not be handled in Solomon's day. But somewhere among those red hills streaked with green, there must be the remnants of Solomon's mine and I would certainly like to find it. Except I don't want to get shot in the process.

TOO MUCH GOVERNMENT IN KIEV
(W. Umbreit)

Which reminds me that I was with a U S government delegation looking into the antibiotic situation in the Soviet Union. There were four of us Americans and we were watched by two Russians. One was a microbiologist (rather ineffective) and the other was a very intelligent and helpful GPU man (the name of the secret service at the time). On this day we were staying in a second rate hotel in Kiev because the major hotel was "undergoing reconstruction" (i.e. they did not want us mingling with the possible tourists in Kiev). I found it difficult to sleep in the hotel because the building vibrated, and one morning I got up real early and went for a walk (unaccompanied, of course). Then I found out what the trouble was. The whole basement of the hotel was occupied by machines, IBM type punched card sorters, and there were so many that they caused the entire building to shake. Of course, if the government does all the business, the government must do all of the accounting.

One sunny afternoon, being unengaged for the moment, we went for a walk, accompanied by our escorts. But it was a nice day and we wandered off in different directions, partly for the consternation of our escorts. As such, I found myself alone walking along the street of downtown Kiev. A sudden shower came up and I dashed for cover into a "stand up" restaurant, a sort of place where there was a counter at which you bought food, and then ate it at stand up benches along the wall and around any supporting pillars. This was the days before 'McDonalds" had invaded the Soviet Union.

While I was eating there, a young man came up to me and wanted to speak to me. He had studied English at Kiev University and this was his first chance to try it on an 'Englishman' (at the time I took this to be authentic, but I have wondered since if it was a plant. Because of the circumstances I do not think so, but if it was, it showed that we were under more intensive scrutiny than we supposed, or indeed than we were worth). His English was not bad and we had a nice conversation, about the weather, and how I liked Kiev all the usual chit chat. But we attracted attention and soon were surrounded by several people. One of them was a very large man who said he was a miner. He said that he had heard that in the U S more and more people were employed by the government. Was this true? I said yes I thought it was true and that if it continued we would have as many people employed by the government as Kiev did (where everybody was so employed). He cursed and said that this was the trouble with Kiev—too many people were employed by the government.

WATCHED BY THE FBI
(W. Umbreit)

Which reminds me, I am sitting in the international section of the airport in Prague, Czechoslovakia, on a Sunday morning waiting for a plane to arrive from Moscow to take me to Moscow. I cannot move outside of the International section since I have no visa for Czechoslovakia, in fact I have been denied one by the Czech (and the Russian) consulates in Vienna. How I got into this fine situation requires a book to explain and some understanding of the bureaucracy of the communist world. But that is for another time. The only reason I am here is that a ticket agent of KLM (the Dutch airline) in Vienna pointed out that the international zone is not in the country so I did not need a visa to get to it. I could stay for 24 hours and while he could get me on the morning KLM flight (essentially the only one into the country) but he could not promise to get me out. Right now I am drinking good Czech beer with an East German, the only other occupant of the international section (it is Sunday and everything, except the bar, is closed). I receive a telegram saying that the people I was to meet in Moscow are stuck in Gander (a stopping point for international flights in those days). I could not go back to Vienna, or any place else for that matter. There were no flights. So, there was no alternative, I would have to go on to Moscow alone. And I did not like the idea. I expressed this to the East German who said I need have no fears. Moscow was a fine city, the beer was good, the people tolerable. When I did not seem to cheer up he said "I know your trouble, you are being watched not only by the KGB (the Russian secret police) but also by the FBI and to his mind, it was the FBI that I should worry about.

SectionFour
THE CAPITAN DISK

A Novelette

(W. Umbreit**)**

I have called this a novelette, if there is such a thing, since it is so short. I don't like to call it a "short story" since this implies sheer fiction, whereas this has some basis if fact, however small. But it is not really related to most novels I have read. It has no love story, no sex, no wild car chases, no shootouts, so how can it be a novel? By this word I mean to imply that it is not all fact. In short, some is fact, some is reasonable conjecture, and some I just made up to make the rest fit. I do not cite sources for some of the facts I mention, because this would make things too complicated and I am not a scholar. In fact, I get bored much too easily. Maybe you will be bored but keep trying for a while. It might be fun.

For me, this story begins with the following newspaper article, which I did not see until two years after it was published; (i.e. 1997)

Capitan, New Mexico Sept 3 1995(AP) There was an enormous explosion at the Iverson ranch this afternoon at the storage silos at the intersections between sections 445, 446, 573, 574, a storage unit exactly in the center of the 1500 acre ranch owned by the Iverson Co. of Philadelphia. The ranch is operated by Mr. Judd Reid on a sharecrop basis who grazes cattle on the area except for the small central area where the storage units are. Here there were two large silos and a scattering of smaller sheds. No one was injured as no one was present in this area at the time. Mr. Reid said that the Iverson Co. stored machinery at the site and that occasionally Iverson personnel would come and work there. There was a mobile home at the site but it was unoccupied when the blast occurred. Mr. Reid lives in a house at the edge of the ranch and was not a witness to the blast."

Naturally, since I live in Evanston, Ill (when I am "home"), what did this have to do with me?. Well, two years later I was handed a computer disk by my boss, Professor Aron, who said that it had been found at Capitan, N. M., and that it seemed to be in ancient Sumarian, or some other lost language. Professor Aron was an expert in old Sumarian and therefore it was sent to him for interpretation, others having failed in the attempt. Of course ancient Sumarian was written in cuneiform script on clay tablets and the disk had letters and symbols on a computer in sort of Arabic but interspersed with symbols, completely incomprehensible. However, the arrangement of the letters and particularly the location of the periods, suggested to some discerning soul that the language may have been derived from ancient Sumarian.

In order to explain what happened further, I must tell you a little about myself and about Professor Aron, not that I am necessarily reluctant to do so, since I am rather proud of what I do, whatever you may think. Professor Aron is a genius, well known in several fields of study but particularly known as a translator of cuneiform script especially Sumarian. He was independently wealthy but became fascinated with scholarship at an early age, traveled the world on various expeditions, but now at the age of about 65 (I never did know exactly) has settled down in a large house in Evanston, on Ridge Avenue—close to the "L" so that we can hear its rumbling. This house is filled with collections of various scripts and also many artifacts which he picked up over the course of the years. One of my jobs is to keep these collections in order, to add to them when possible, to authenticate any whose ancestry may be questionable, and in general to do any of the errands assigned to me. I am happy to do this since Professor Aron is not only a genius but a very kind and understanding gentleman. Like many wealthy persons he has little regard for cost, so he pays me an excellent salary and a free spending expense account. He sends me on trips to various parts of the world, mostly to look at something that has come to his attention (he hates to travel at his age). Frequently, if I judge the find to be authentic, I am empowered to negotiate for it. I can stay at the best hotels, but if I am negotiating for an object, I usually don't, since it gives the seller the idea that we are rich (which we are) and thus there is a tendency on his part to get stubborn about the price. But when I am not negotiating, just searching, I stay at the very best, Aron insists on it, and it is indeed nice, after a day of scrounging in the souks or bazaars or the pawnshops and flea markets, to come back to a western type civilized hotel.

I am not really qualified for this job. I speak only English (of a type), a little German, less Russian and a smattering of half a dozen other tongues—sometimes mostly variants of Spanish. I first met Professor Aron just after I graduated from college (majoring in Chemistry!) and attended a lecture of his on Sumarian Art, why I'll never know. Now Aron thought faster than he could speak and I had the happy facility of speaking faster than I thought so I could finish sentences for him while he started on the next. If my interpretation was correct he would nod and we would proceed. A conversation between us consisted of us both talking at the same time, with much head nodding, but it went on quite well. He hired me, right off, as a chemist to look into the silicate composition of some of the Sumarian tablets in an effort to establish their origin. I did not accomplish much, my college training was not adequate for the task. Like most college chemistry, it taught me a lot about electrons but little about electricity or how to deal with the complexities of silicon, but Professor Aron and I got along well. He is a rather shy person and does not thrive on personal contact. As such, being a brash and confident young man, I soon took over his public relations problems. I have the happy facility of getting along with lots of different people, aristocrats and beggars, holy men and thieves, and I evidently easily establish a relationship with them, not really of friendship but with the general feeling that we all can get along with each other. This has been very helpful to me but with it came the good sense not to let it get out of hand, and if I got into situations beyond my depth, to be very discreet until I got out of them and could get to the source of information I needed to make a good showing. Professor Aron was most helpful in this respect, and gradually I got more confidence and skill.

So now I had a computer disk in undecipherable symbols and I had to figure out how to read it, knowing only a few modern languages and not a single ancient one. I first went to a friend of mine (I almost said Charley Chan) whose name is really Charles Fan and who is a computer whiz with a great sense of humor. Dr. Fan (as he is formally known) took the disk for about a week and then called me. He said that he was making some progress but could I get him a copy of an ancient Sumarian script both in cuneiform and in English letters so that he could make some comparisons? Of course, Professor Aron gave me such a script, a translation into English letters (where possible) together with his translation into modern English—which was the first time I heard of the ancient Sumarian legends of the origins of mankind. I'll quote this translation (or at least a paraphrase of it, Aron tends to be wordy) later. Within a week Fan was back with a disk which gave the equivalent of the letters and symbols into English letters which of course, neither he nor I could interpret. Professor Aron went to work and by the end of a month had produced an English language version of the text of the disk. From what we read here, we dropped everything else and started to look at the material on this disk. So this is how it started.

I have mentioned that Prof. Aron is an expert at deciphering cuneform writing. That simple statement is much too modest. If you, like me, happen to know little about cuneform except that it was made up of little triangular marks made in clay which is then baked, you will (like me) be surprised as to how complex reading cuneiform can become.

Working for Prof. Aron, as I do, I gradually got to be more familiar with this work (I never took to it) and I was really impressed.

So I thought you might like to know how really difficult it is. The figure shows a cuneiform script just as it comes from the clay tablet.

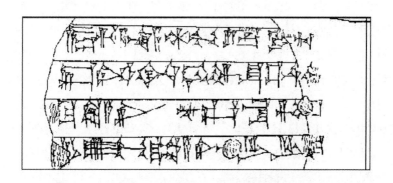

This comes out in English letters as:
ukur-rea-na-ammu-un-tur-ree-na$_4$-kin-na
gu-im-su-rin-na-kam
tug-bir$_7$-a-ninu-kal-la-ge-[da]mnig-u-gu-de-a-ninu-kin-kin-d[a]m

This has been translated as:
How lowly is the poor man,
His work is at the edge of the oven,
His ripped garments will not be mended,
What he has lost will not be sought for.

There are thousands of such tablets, mostly dealing with commercial transactions or property deeds, but some containing poetry (as the above) or philosophy, and some even history. Thank goodness I don't have to spend my time trying to read it.

I will now start to quote the disk, or rather what Fan and Aron said was there. It appears to be a message, left for the instruction of some incoming passenger as to how to get along in the modern world. Presumably this passenger was coming from somewhere in space. It was evidently written by a person who had himself faced these problems without sound advice from his predecessor. He goes into great detail about some of the problems encountered, but seems to ignore others that we would think might be formidable (i.e., how does one make contact with and gain the assistance of strangers?). He evidently does not know the background of the incoming passenger except that he comes from an elite class. The material on the disk seems all too human. This kind of knowledge is very useful to us, since we were unaware that anything of this sort existed. Having dealt in a world sometimes subject to fraud, we were always looking for clues as to the authenticity of the work, and here was a good chance to exercise our skills. So we began to look at this information in some detail. To avoid confusion, I shall print the quotations from the disk in italics and underlined. This permits you to see what the disk actually contained. Of course, this is our translation of it and there may be some errors in our interpretation. The material actually on the disk we print in italics with underline.

Welcome to the new world. While our people have been in contact with this world for many years and we have accumulated much information about it, it is difficult to express how rapidly it has changed even in the time since I have been here and time is so short between the time we meet and we both must be off, that I thought to give you some useful information. You should first know that 1 year to us is equivalent to 10 earth years. They count the time from sunrise to sunrise such days to encircle their sun. When we came we agreed to stay here one year (10 years their time) and on your trip to the moon station you have practiced (I hope) the earth day routine. Their day is *thus about half the length of the days we got used to on Mars, before it blew up, of course. After this, except where mentioned, I will refer to earth years, earth days, etc. since you need to get used to this short cycle*

Here on earth most people live 60-70 years (aged 6-7 our scale) and very few reach 10 (compared to our 40 years of life = 400 earth years). (The old Sumarian legends speak of people living an average of 400 years and the Bible, possibly derived from the Sumarian legends, speaks of people with very long lives as Abraham (175 yrs.), Noah (950 yrs.) Methuselah (969 yrs.) etc.).

As such it is proper for us to be of the age of 3 to 4 (our years) since the adults who are responsible for the conduct of life here are 30-40 earth years old. Fortunately, we look enough like most of them (although with smoother skin) that we can pass reasonably well. After all they are descended, in a sense, from us. Do not, however, go out into the country or especially the cities, until two or three weeks have passed at our earth station and you get used to the manner of dress and more especially the manner of speaking used by the people of this world. Unfortunately our earth station is in a sparsely populated area of a large country (called United States) in a state called New Mexico, and their manner of speech is somewhat different from the rest of the country—so pass yourself off as Hispanic—that is American Spanish or Mexican—who are not really expected to speak properly anyway. To do that, try to learn a little Spanish; the best source is from the employees of the Iverson Company who will be there to assist you until you are ready to venture into the new world. They do not generally speak anything but the most rudimentary English (the language you have been taught)—but the English you have been taught does not bear too much of a relation to that spoken in the streets. Further, it changes and even the "hip" language that I had to learn ("hip" means "up to date" which means proper for the time) will be replaced by new "catch phrases" (= words that convey a special meaning somewhat independent of their *actual meaning).For example the word "cool" means "I like that" or "its fine" rather than coldness. As such, as you first venture out, you must be careful to talk only when necessary and listen carefully to the language as spoken.*

In spite of the language difficulties mentioned we have moved our earth station from what is called the "Middle East" to the United States, which, while a large country, is not the largest, but it does have, as of the time I have been there (their count 1981-1991) the most influence in the world and if it becomes necessary for us to colonize the earth, this country is where we should start.

We have seen references on the disk to earlier times, so perhaps now is the time to summarize what Professor Aron retrieved from the ancient cuneiform documents that he had previously investigated. According to this theory (which I have put into bold type to emphasize that it does not come from the disk but was deduced from the cuneiform tablets— some years before we had knowledge of the disk, but which makes interpretation of the disk more interesting.)

About 12,000 years ago, some creatures traveled from across the vastness of space, using some unknown power, and found a satellite of the sun (which the primitive inhabitants called "earth") which had the conditions required for their sustenance and survival. The myth says that they were searching for gold which they needed to protect their home from ozone in the air, but that seems unlikely. At any rate they found a primitive creature living on this earth which creature was closely related to the other animals—more particularly the chimpanzee—but the creature lacked any appreciable reasoning power and was only slowly evolving into a thinking being. By way of what is now called genetic engineering (only recently discovered) these foreign beings introduced the genes for intelligence into this creature and he became very useful in constructing the things they wanted or needed to build. These were presumably the pyramids (as markers for their spacecraft) and the landing fields at what is now called Balbeck. This happening is preserved in their myths. In a book called the Bible it is described as "eating from the tree of knowledge of good and evil". The beings from space were known by earth "men" as very superior creatures—they called them "Gods". There were several such gods—one of which, named YAHWA, became the god of the people we know today as Hebrew.

Note: Evidence shows that the pyramids and certain large buildings at Giza, Heliopolis, and Lebanon are much older than the age attributed to them by the usual chronology (i.e. They are 8-10,000 BC; not the 3-4000 usually ascribed to them). I can provide very good evidence for this. One example shows that the Sphinx has weathered from water running off it for many, many years, yet there had been no water of that proportion in the period of known history starting at 3,700 BC.

Things went quite well and these beings were seriously considering moving to this planet when the ground shifted, and the inhabitable regions turned cold (what they call the "ice" age). The beings left on their space ships but the capacity of such ships was limited and some were left behind. After about 1000 years (100 years their time) it warmed up again but now there was a great flood which wiped out all the inhabitants ("gods" and men)—except a very few who lived on the high mountains. There are stories of some who survived in boats (one has been called Noah). At any rate a new set of beings landed again about 6000 BC (8000 earth years ago) and started over. The survivors had some intelligence and were soon building the country again. The visiting beings built several more cities and established a flourishing country. Unfortunately a squabble broke out among them. The human population, knowing no better. was divided between them. Several wars were fought. In the final war, an atomic bomb (as they call it) was released at what is now Baghdad and the radioactivity spread throughout the large sea area and most humans died off. As intruders we had to leave the area immediately and take our ships back home. Some few humans survived and started again. Some of these possessed an excellent memory and began to build homes, farms and cities on a large river that ran north (the country is now called Egypt; the river, (the Nile) and also on the great plains to the north between two large rivers that started in the mountains (where some had survived) called the Tigris and Euphrates rivers. They developed a magnificent civilization, its chief city being Sumer.

This is the Sumarian myth somewhat paraphrased as Professor Aron developed it out of the clay tablets of Sumer. Echoes of this myth are found in the epic of Gilgamesh and in the Bible. It is well to know this background, certainly part of the knowledge of the people of the disk, since it becomes easier to interpret why they did some of the things they did. It is also part of the scenario I have proposed.

To return to the translation of the disk:

We were discouraged from settling or moving to earth since the radiation level was still high but we visited it with delegations (such as the one you are on) about every 10 years (100 years their time). In the meantime, over the centuries, life at our home improved and we no longer wanted to live on earth, but were still interested to see what was going on. We observed, and possibly had something to do with, two developments which changed the earth. One, about 400-500 BC was the establishment of an organized so called "Roman Empire", which ruled the world (at least that part they knew about). It turned out that they later found out about the two other civilizations we had established, the oriental or Chinese, and the Indian continent. About 100 earth years ago some unusual things began to happen on earth, so we increased our visits to 10 earth years starting about 1871 by their count.(This is 120 years (2 X 60) before the last launch of the supply ship (1931). They count years from the birth of a prophet they call "Christ" (some use other dates). Today we send four space ships and observers, one to the orient-China and Japan, another to India and the central Asia area, and a third to the mid-east, the Arab countries. The Arab countries date time from a different prophet, one Mohammed who was born ca 582 on the Arabian peninsula. In 622 he began to expound a new religion so these people count time from then, i.e. today (1995) would be 1353. Incidentally, Mohammed, at age 40, claimed to have been visited by the archangel Gabriel. I would be interested to know if this was one of us. I don't remember seeing this in the records, but when I return I will surely look it up. If some delegate did so reveal himself or was trapped into such admission, he would probably keep it quiet. The fourth mission is to the United States.

From the United States we can also monitor the area known as Europe since the ties are very close. I will not know, till I get back, what the results of the delegations to the other areas may be and what I tell you here may or may not apply to them. Since we will not have time to discuss this during the exchange on the space ship I am putting these on com-

puter disk. Clearly I have had to improvise since their computers do not have a font of our language, but I hope that my use of the English letters and some symbols will not be too difficult for you to unscramble. You may as well get used to the earth-type computer since it is almost an essential part of your daily life here.

To live on earth we need money. To carry out our mission we can get along on $ 40,000 a year but it is better to plan on having $ 60,000 plus what we may make by way of work or deals or even bribes. As you know we pay for this by trading Matus which the earth people call diamonds. They are very abundant at home and can be picked up with sound-shovels at the beach at Matu. They make nice decorations for jewelry and since they are very hard, they also serve in a variety of places where their hardness is helpful. On earth diamonds are rather scarce. Only about 20% of those found or mined are suitable for gems. The stones cut for jewelry are the only ones considered here since these are the only ones we bring. Our methods of cutting and polishing are so much better than those *on earth, that it is convenient to bring the finished jewels. They are sold here by the carat which is 0.2 gram in weight, i.e. there are 5 carats in one gram. There are five classes of clarity—FS (flawless), VVS (very, very small inclusions), VS (very small inclusions), SI (small inclusions) and "11, 12, 13" (inclusions). Now the VVS and the VS are jewel quality and most diamonds so used are of this category. While we have lots of FS stones, we do not bring many of these since it would be suspicious if the market were suddenly flooded with these. The VVS stones (cut and polished but unset) sell for about $ 600 per carat (at wholesale level). Rather than get into the diamond market which is a traitorous area in itself, we go through trusted dealers and sell for about $ 500 per carat or $ 2000 per gram. To provide the cash required ($ 60,000) we thus need 30 grams/year or 300 grams for the ten year period. This amount is easily carried in the pocket and easily stashed away on arrival. Do not sell all the diamonds at the start. Sell maybe 10 grams ($20,000 or more) at suitable intervals. The best way I have* *found to do this is through the Iverson company with whom we have a contract to run our ranch in New Mexico where we have our earth station landing site. The Iverson company of Philadelphia is a land and real estate company. But the Iverson Company of New York is the Iverson Diamond Exchange and has branches in Chicago and San Francisco. I started there with a Mr. John J. Cohen and found him very satisfactory. He was honest with me (I think) and since he made quite a bit of money off of our transactions, he was always trying to get the best possible price for them. He worked on a commission of 12%. It shows you how little I know of the diamond market that I don't know whether this was high or low. I pretended to be an engineer from North West Brazil (where there are diamond mines) which accounted for my supply of diamonds as well as my curious accent.*

My story was that I was shipped these diamonds periodically by my Uncle who owned a mine in the proper area. He never asked if I spoke Portuguese. When he retired I was inherited by a Mr. Saul Hurwitz, who was much more curious and was skeptical of my story. Eventually I convinced him that it was at least partially true, and since he made money from the deals, he agreed to market the Matus for me. I also set up accounts at banks in New York, Chicago, and San Francisco and rented a small savings deposit box at each bank where I stored the unsold diamonds. I further obtained "credit cards" under three different names from three different companies. (Visa, Master Card, and American Express). It is remarkable how easy these are to obtain and how little information one need supply, providing that one has a checking, or savings, account at a respectable bank and providing one pays up the charges on time (although you would think that the card companies would want you to be delinquent since they can then charge enormous interest and late payment fines). I did not rent apartments in my three main cities but rather had a room (in Chicago, three rooms) in a residential hotel. I put out that I was a traveling man. Since I had some experience in geology I said that I was an independent oil geologist. This seemed to work. You must pick a cover suitable to your education and inclinations, but just be sure that you know something about the subject since you can easily be betrayed by lack of knowledge or lack of response to something "known by everyone" in the field, although never necessarily mentioned outright. For the rest, try to blend in; don't dress in the latest fashion, but as an average man in your chosen profession might dress, etc. Do not spend too freely or you will be cheated yet do not depend on the payment of others: pay your share of the expenses with as good a grace as you can, There is sometimes a delicate balance that needs to be observed. Entertain carefully and then on a small scale. You can learn more from an intimate dinner with three or four friends, carefully chosen, than at a large cocktail party, where you may talk with 50 people. Much of what you may overhear there is nonsense; things said mostly to be polite. Do not get into arguments or quarrels.

In the course of time, you will probably hear or participate in discussions of space travel. Never—Never-- Never admit that you have so traveled. These people know nothing about the power of synchronous sound. We used it in the early days to build the pyramids but we never told them what it was or how to use it. Don't you tell them either. Every once in a while by accident, they make use of it; Joshua at the walls of Jericho, for example, but they have no idea that they are using a natural force. They do not know of the ways of space travel. Only now some of their mathematics people are talking about "liberation points" and "manifolds" but they have no idea as to how to use them properly.

I have asked my astronomer friends to explain these to me. Some had never heard of them, but I got the general idea that "liberation points" are some kind of a mathematical calculation as to where "lines of force" (whatever they are) come together and at such points all forces cancel. When you arrive at such a point, you can stay there forever with no expenditure of energy and you can surf from one liberation point to another with very little expenditure of either time or energy. Sounds peculiar to me. Now "manifolds" are supposed to be a kind of matrix of space which, if you know how to follow them, permits movement through space, or at least arrival at a desired destination, much more rapidly. Clearly I don't understand this, so I am not able to explain it adequately.

And food—don't ever tell them how you were fed during the 10 years you traveled from home to earth. On earth most people eat three meals a day. One, when they get up (not necessarily sunrise) called "breakfast". Another, larger meal at mid-day (midday is called "noon"; the meal is called lunch or dinner) and another, usually a large meal, in the evening (called dinner or supper). The language can get confusing for logical types like ourselves. You will simply have to get used to this and to the things they eat. There are several types of cultures and customs in any country and the nature of the food varies also. Take what you get and try to enjoy it. You really can't change it and you must eat, as they say *"to keep body and soul together"* which means not to die, soul being the *"spirit"* that invades and lives in the body, the conscious part of the brain.

Now you have landed from the moon station after a voyage of 10 years (earth time) moving at 82% of the speed of light. This means that you are 8.2 light years from home. Communication across this distance is rather slow so you cannot get advice from home (unless you have access to the instrumentation at New Mexico, which you will have only for a short time) and that advice, after going through the countless committees, is outdated and probably useless anyway. Also remember that the moon ship can stay in the dark of the moon no more than three days without a serious risk of detection. It has probably been detected but its existence is so unlikely, in the philosophy of even their most advanced citizens, that those who proclaim to have seen *"alien space ships"* are regarded as *"somewhat off the beam"* (it will be a good exercise to try to figure out what this means, in fact even *"figure out"* may cause some difficulty). This is your intro-

duction to the language of the day, quite different from the language that was transmitted back to home 10 years ago, assimilated and taught to you for 10 years and then transmitted via you back to earth = 30 years out of date (earth years, of course).

Incidentally, our earth station is located about 30 miles northeast of Capitan, New Mexico, which is about 50 miles from Roswell, New Mexico. Roswell has become something of a tourist attraction because UFO's have been sighted there. UFO stands for Unidentified Flying Object. Evidently at one time or another our small space craft have been detected due to some reflection or something of the sort since they are otherwise invisible. The earth people are becoming more sophisticated in their instrumentation. They even have a great many small objects circulating the earth (and a few much farther out) so that it is becoming increasingly difficult to navigate to our moon site without encountering them. Before long, I am afraid, we will no longer be able to operate without their knowledge. I have urged the Enil-Ki in my reports to reveal our presence now while we still have the advantage over them and so that we can take advantage of their system of implementing new ideas which I will discuss later. So far no response. But do not go to Roswell. Not that you would be recognized, but to avoid any suggestion that you are aware of a space culture. Further, New Mexico is a state in the country, the United States. There is a country to the south, called Mexico. Do not get them confused.

It seems from this and other hints on the disk, that these creatures (men) live on a "planet 8.2 light years from earth. This planet evidently orbits a "sun", which seems to be about 0.5 of a light year away from it. The "sun would thus be 8.7 light years from us. I have asked my astronomer friends whether this is possible. They say that there is a star, Sirius, which is 8.7 light years away. This star has been known for millennia. The Egyptians worshiped it as a god. It is the brightest star in the sky. It has one and possibly two moons, none capable of sustaining life as we know it and since the persons here are passing among us

240

as men, they must be much like us. I have asked, as discreetly as I could, where there could be a planet, much like ours, rotating in an elliptical orbit around Sirius without us being aware of it. The answers I get, as far as I understand them, range from a resounding "not possible" (older more experienced astronomers) to "well there is a remote chance". Knowing no astronomy and frequently confused by geometrical concepts, I have gone to the mythical literature and to the ancient tales (even the Bible) and come up with about the following picture. Professor Aron says that this is interesting but that he could not sponsor it.

I suppose that there is a planet orbiting around the star Sirius at about one-half a light year distant from it at its closest point. So much energy is generated by Sirius that closer contact would be impossible for a planet much like ours. This planet comes to the same point in its orbit every 60 years. Some older religions celebrate the arrival of Sirius every 60 years (the last being in 1931). There is much information in the ancient litera-

ture which postulates a 60 year cycle. We even use the 60 unit system (which originated, I think, in the ancient city of Sumer) for time (minutes, seconds) and for angular measurements (degrees of a circle=6 x 60's). I postulate that from this planet, a space station is launched every 60 years when it is closest to the earth (and receiving the most energy from its star).

The astronomy and the space calculations get to me. I have spent hours calculating how it can be done, but it seems futile to one of my background, so I will omit it.

There is still more information on the disk:

As you know for thousands of years we were way ahead of the earth people. We had space ships, computers, good food, etc. They seemed to be going nowhere in spite of the intelligence we gave them. They just couldn't seem to make it work. Shortly after the last time we landed our delegation of 60 (in 1881), things began to change, very slowly at first, but more and more rapidly as the years went by. You have seen how they have put up satellites into space, so many that it is becoming difficult to get to our moon hideout without running into them. Indeed, they now have means to detect us which never existed before. What I fear is that in the next ten years, when you are on earth, they may reach our state of development, and even surpass it. I cannot put this fear into reports. Its cause, I believe, is a peculiar organization, or perhaps lack of organization which has developed in certain parts of the earth. It involves very few people, but the results of their work affect millions who may not even understand what is going on. This organization is entirely against our concepts of order, but, unfortunately, it seems to work, however confused and wasteful it is. You can imagine the concern if I were to mention this in the formal report. But I would like you to look at this problem, and see if you agree. If so, when you return we will both go to Enil-Ki and tell him what we conclude. If you can provide concrete evidence of the change in earth's potential, so much the better. Of course you may disagree with me, in which case we need go no further.

When we first landed on earth, in about 12,000 BC and gave man the "knowledge of good and evil" i.e. a certain intelligence, we also imparted our method of organization. There was a ruler Enil-Ki who held all power. Helping him was a court composed mostly of his sons, daughters, and close relatives. These were called royalty. As populations grew, the court did too, but not nearly as fast as the non-royal people They were therefore organized into nobles (not royal but closely related), superiors, servants, peasants. We never used slaves although the earth organizations which were, of course, patterned after ours, did employ a lower class who had very few privileges. We depended for our progress on a series of nobles and superiors who ran laboratories and research institutes and found out many things about the universe which were very useful to us. For 14,000 earth years we were greatly in advance of earth and their progress seemed to be so slow that we had to come down about every 3,600 years and start it again. But about 1750 things began to change. An idea was hatched that there did not have to be this kind or organization. Instead there should be a different kind which provided what was called "freedom" which to us looked like chaos and really was. This is not to say that our organization did not persist. Indeed there are some countries where the government is still organized on this basis. One of the strong organizations still based on our system is the main church, which is devoted to worshiping us (as gods) which is the way we were thought of when men first encountered us.

Now this idea of freedom, let each man be the best he can, began slowly to take hold. After a century or so, men of common stock (not of superior stock) had devised systems which improved their world. They invented "mass production" which made things available to many people, not just the few privileged. By 1871 they had developed a power to move people and supplies about the country with adequate speed. These devices, railroads and steam ships, depended on heat power, properly harnessed, of course. The point was that they had developed the abilities to conceive of such things and to actually build them. Their next step in the early 1900's was to develop electrical power, electric motors, radio, television. And simultaneously they developed power sources using petroleum and this changed their ability to move people and supplies, cars and trucks. Today every family has a least one car and life is inconceivable without it. All of this was normal development, much as we went through earlier.

This development is abnormal. So I have tried to find out why, after so many centuries of stagnation with slow and almost imperceptible progress, there should suddenly be this remarkable advance so that improvements which took centuries now occur in decades. There are, on earth, three systems of organization for people (incidentally there are almost 3 billion people now on earth). One is an organization much like ours, patterned after ours, of course. Its example is called absolute monarchy. The catholic church has such an organization. There is a "pope" who has absolute power. Whatever he wishes is done. Of course, such being their nature (derived from us) that over the course of time this absolute power is somewhat diluted. The pope has absolute power but he is surrounded by a "college" of cardinals who see to it that he doesn't use it. A second type of organization is the planned society, a good example is the communist system. The idea here is that everyone should work for the common good. The "state" will decide what should be done, will plan on how to do it, and everybody will work to see that the proper thing is done. An example is the communist state of the Soviet Union, a group of "states" united for this purpose. This system failed because it was soon taken over by promoters and dictators and became like a monarchy except that its leaders were chosen not by birth, but by political expediency. It was the planning part of the idea that was particularly bad. Planning became the prerogative of a special group, who planned things for their own benefit, but it took months and years for a new, and possibly valuable idea or invention to actually be used or exploited. Initially, the system worked fairly well but as time went on and lines of power became established, new ideas were not really welcomed and the tried and true methods were employed. Eventually this led to complete stagnation. There was a joke: we pretend to work; you pretend to pay us and the system finally collapsed during the time I was here. Now we are such a monarchy influenced by the planning aspect of the communistic system. So long as the system is young, it is productive, as witness our enormous advances centuries ago. But such a system can stagnate, and a bureaucracy develops which enforces a particular viewpoint—one must be "politically correct" to prosper. I think that you will recognize that we are in somewhat that condition today. There have been no really revolutionary changes in our society for 100 of our years (1000 of the earth years).

During that time, society on earth has progressed much more rapidly then we. Certain parts of the earth system are organized on a somewhat different basis. There is a good deal of rhetoric and hullabaloo about this, and much hypocrisy, but the essential idea is that power comes, not from god, or from his personal representative, the king, but from the people. They decide what should be done. Now, to get any group larger than 5 to agree on anything important, or anything new, is almost impossible so while there are books of laws, and regulations, there is much that cannot be so controlled. Each individual can go his own way, within limits. But these limits are not only "law" and custom, but economic and social conditions. However, there is also the general idea that "laws are made to be broken", one should question each pronouncement and test it to see if it is correct. In short, if an idea occurs to you, do not discard it out of hand, but if it seems possible, try it. Maybe you can make money on it, and thus improve your condition. Now this approach is available not just to an educated class, but to everyone, no matter how much of a "screwball" or "nerd" he may be (try to find out what these mean).

They don't have an "educated class" as we do. All of the children are sent to school until the age of 18. Then a reasonable proportion go on to "higher education", much of it supported at random by the state. The universities themselves, where much of this education takes place, are both pillars of the current philosophy (to an outsider, one rarely hears that much nonsense purveyed as fact or "scholarly consensus") and sources of innovation. Some of the material expounded is so absurd that even the half-awake student begins to wonder where this can be so. If he has enough initiative he can not only question the dogma, but can actually try out some new idea. Now all of this is common even in our system. But what is different here is that there are thousands and thousands of such innovators, trying out a broad array of somewhat "off beat" ideas (another of their strange words). And they can try them out. They don't have to go to some committee. Sometimes individuals and even government divisions will finance their efforts or they can pay for them themselves. Out of these mil-

lions of trials, even if not sponsored, some work and some of these can be exploited, some even make money by doing things better or more quickly or at less cost, and some even do things that have never been done before. The method seems disorganized and wasteful. Indeed it is.

Much useful information lies buried in the minds or experiences of individuals and others are never aware of it. But sometime, "when the time is ripe" (who ever heard of green or ripe time?) this fact may be discovered again and be of great use. It is just this that permits such rapid advance, based upon experiences already incorporated into knowledge being improved and modified for other purposes. This is the story of their computers which are becoming better than ours. Originally they were just more complex calculating machines; then they began to treat words and sentences, then complex mathematical concepts, then they were able to communicate with each other. A "network" was established and today literally millions of people can communicate instantaneously with each *other all over the world with just a rather inexpensive piece of machinery and a keyboard and this information can be saved, retrieved, modified and organized. Not only is this exceedingly useful. After all, this disk saves and passes on to you, what I regard as important information but also permits you, not only to contemplate this information but to modify it, to alter it, and to destroy it, if you wish. It even corrects your spelling. Of course, such a network contains a lot of non-sense and considerable misinformation not to mention thieves and crooks of various sorts. And most of this is driven, not by a deep desire for knowledge, but for financial gain, a far stronger motive. As such, rather than depend on a small circle of "elite" minds who tend to become more rigid and less excited by new ideas as they grow older, we have the thoughts of literally thousands of fresh minds, from which, in our more mature wisdom we can pick out and try those ideas that might work to solve the problem or improve the situation we are faced with. I would urge you to particularly evaluate this approach to see if we can-*

not introduce it, with suitable modification for our superior technology, into our own system so that we can again make rapid progress beyond that of our knowledge of the past and thus stay ahead of the earthlings. It is clear, I think, that I am afraid that they will approach our knowledge or even exceed it.

One other aspect, I should like you to look at. Being human and somewhat related to us, they don't get along too well, and various disputes arise and frequently these result in war. Normally, this is regarded as a great evil, and certainly it does result in personal tragedy. But in one sense war does serve two useful functions.

One, it tends to reduce the populations whose breeding capabilities are using up the natural resources of the earth. But the other, less well recognized, is that war stimulates innovation. So anxious is one side to defeat its opponents that they will think up and test out any idea that might be useful, almost independently of the cost. As such, after every war, even in countries and cities devastated by the conflict, a resurgence and application of war developed ideas to normal life. The computer networks are an example of this. What we need to do, is to provide this same stimulus without war's destruction. Can you devise a way to do it, within the structure of our society, of course? When you return I would be most interested in your conclusions and being a member of the very small group that has had first hand experience with the earth, maybe we can do something to improve our own. Clearly I may have been on earth too long.

This is the end of the disk. Clearly the writer has the benefit of a long period of observation. He has made some rather shrewd observations about our society. His comparisons with the society he came from tell us a great deal about it, as well. He speaks with a certain authority. He has the outlook of a trained sociologist. I found his comments especially stimulating. But part of the problem with them is "are they really authentic?" Was there a person from another culture in space, who was landed on earth and observed the changes which occurred from about 1935 to 1995? If so, perhaps he was more aware of them than we were, living amongst the changes, and actually trying to use them to our individual advantage. Maybe we missed the bigger picture which was unfolding and which is so succinctly described on this disk. Why was it recorded in such a peculiar language? That is, a mixture of archaic English with a set of symbols most of which were somewhat familiar to Aron. Presumably the person to whom it was addressed, the next 60-year observer, would speak English, after all he had to pass as a native of the earth. Why could the message not be formulated in normal English? I asked the computer expert, Dr. Fan, about this and he suggested that it might take some time for the new visitor to get used to and be able to use our computers (which the people from space would know little about since it was 60 years since they had last made contact) and maybe it had to be formulated in this fashion so that it would fit with the 'space' computer which the new observer would presumably be carrying. We were, and still are, puzzled by this, but it was indeed written, so far as we could tell, this is what it said. It was somewhat cruder and I have polished it a bit to make it easier to read.

The disk ends very abruptly, almost as if the writer was interrupted. Clearly we don't know what happened. Dr. Fan went out to the Iverson ranch in Capitan. He met Mr. Reid who proved to be a pleasant but rather laconic westerner. Posing as an insurance inspector he searched the remains without finding anything. Part of the mobile home was still standing and in it was a battered computer but it had nothing on its hard disk and other storage units, such as 'My Documents' were empty. There were some marks on these items but we could retrieve nothing and Dr. Fan is an expert on such retrieval and recovery. As I said, I make quite a few judgments on authenticity or fraud so maybe I am somewhat qualified to evaluate this disk. But honestly, I don't know. One possible idea was that the writer, who was planning to return to his planet, and was leaving helpful instructions for his replacement, was eliminated when the landing spacecraft went wrong and burst into flames, destroying the silos and part of the mobile home and the writer, all that survived was the disk. Such a scenario seems likely to be fiction; indeed one could almost bet on it. Yet it has about it some elements of truth, which are not really known to most investigators (only my association with Prof. Aron provided some insights) and while there are some glitches it seems to be naively honest. But, as I said, we were busy and never did anything more about it.

In the spring of 1999, I was in Chicago attending a meeting and auction of Arabic manuscripts from the library at Timbuktu, at the LaSalle Hotel. While going to lunch I saw in the window of a jewelry shop some curious rock crystals. They were clearly melted on one side, but the other sides had cut faces. I went in an inquired about them since maybe Prof. Aron, who had an interest in odd rock formations, might like these. I was told that these were not quartz, as I assumed, but diamond. Further, that they had been obtained from the Iverson Diamond Exchange. I called Aron in Evanston, told him the story and quoted the rather excessive price, and he said get them. So I got them at somewhat of a discount since while diamonds, they had been damaged. I then took them to Iverson and asked about the origin. They looked it up and said that they had been obtained from a Mr. Reid in New Mexico, but they knew nothing further about them, nor why they were in such "bad shape". Posing as a diamond dealer, I asked to see the appraiser and was soon talking to a Mr. Saul Hurwitz, whose name I remembered from the Capitan Disk. After a brief discussion, Mr. Hurwitz said that we could dispense with all the sparring and get directly to the point since I was wearing the seal and he had instructions to immediately accommodate anyone showing the seal. I was at a loss, until I realized that he was looking at my ring. This was a ring given to me by Prof. Aron showing the bird or eagle or what-ever, which is used in some religious ceremonies but which is common in old Sumarian documents. I therefore ques-tioned Mr. Hurwitz more closely as to why he respected the seal, since it was not Jewish at all, but Sumarian. He said that he did not know what it was, but that his predecessor, J. J. Cohen, had told him that this was company policy which he had received from <u>his</u> predecessor. Since this corresponded with some information on the Capitan Disk, I had some further conversation with Mr. Hurwitz, asking him if the seal was ever used much. He said that he had only one contact who ever used it, a man by the name of Anton Meilke, who usually brought him diamonds from his uncle's mine in Brazil. He told me that Mr. Meilke was a rather tall, thin, man with a sallow, almost greenish complexion, almost completely bald, who spoke English with a Spanish-type accent (possibly Brazilian). I felt that I had gone far enough and not wishing to get into things I didn't understand, I said goodbye and returned to Evanston with the deformed diamonds. Prof. Aron was delighted, although I thought that I had paid too much for the diamonds. But he immediately set to work examining them. He said that the cut faces were VS quality and that the uncut part was due to melting at very high heat.

Prof. Aron wanted to examine the diamonds further but particularly wanted to find how and where they were found. so he sent me to interview Mr. Reid. I flew to Roswell, rented a car at Roswell. From Roswell I called Mr. Reid, who reluctantly agreed to meet me at the ranch, although it was their busy season. I got there about 10:30 A.M.

I wore my ring but did not mention it. Yet as soon as he saw it he was most accommodating. Yes, he said he had found some curious stones near the site of the explosion and on taking it to Iverson, he found that they were worth quite a bit, being partially melted diamonds. He had searched further, far and wide, but had only found a very few others and all in a small area about 4 ft. in diameter. I thought it would be sensible to visit the area, but they were so busy with the round-up that the visit to the area was put off till the next afternoon. Before I returned to Roswell for the night, I saw some of his crew, and among them was a rather short, thin man with a sort of greenish complexion who was completely bald and had a large scar on his right cheek. I attempted conversations with the crew, just to be friendly-like, but this man said not a word. I telephoned Aron that night telling him of my reactions and he told me to see what I could find out about the thin man.

The next morning I went out to the Iverson Ranch getting there about 10 A.M. There was nobody in sight but I finally found the crew working on the "south 40" as they called it. There were seven of them in addition to Mr. Reid, all mounted on horses and dashing about madly, I thought, although there must have been some sense to their activities. There was also sort of a "lunch wagon" but nobody was attending to it. I watched them work for the morning and at about noon they assembled near the lunch wagon. "Bo" was the name they gave to the thin fellow who did not speak. He came in first and heated up some soup and beans and a kind of sausage which they all seemed to relish. I tried to talk to "Bo" but he would not say a word. I had the impression that he partly understood me and seemed to be somewhat alert when I spoke in my Midwestern twang, somewhat different from the southwestern drawl of his teammates and boss. It turned out that the crew all lived at the Reid house near the edge of the property and about 4:30 we all returned there. There seemed to be a lady housekeeper and cook and a large meal was served in a low building called the bunkhouse. I took Mr. Reid out to dinner, however, and we went down to Alamogordo. We had a hearty if rather chewy meal and had a chance to talk, mostly about their type of ranching, with which I was not at all familiar. The crew was mostly Mexican, probably full of illegal immigrants, and was not a permanent crew but of the seven members only three were permanent, meaning that they were there the year around. If a man worked at a place for over seven months, and stayed out of trouble, he was regarded as "permanent". One of these was "Bo", which surprised me since he seemed to be less efficient, although he seemed to fit in fairly well.

I asked Reid about "Bo" and he said that he had been there for three years, never having left the ranch in all that time. Reid said that "Bo" was sort of a charity case and he got a stipend from the state welfare unit which paid part of "Bo's" rather meager salary. I was told that "Bo" had been found about 4 years ago in a rather large pond somewhat to the west of the ranch. He had been spotted by a truck driver coming down US 54 from Santa Rosa to Carrizozo. The presence of a large pond surprised me in such an arid country but there seemed to be several small rivers and after all some 100 miles to the west is the origin of the Rio Grande and there is even a "Bottomless Lakes Park". He also seemed to have been burned, but no one could figure out how, unless the truck on which he was riding caught fire and he had jumped off. He was clearly at deaths door and was not expect to live. In about a week he came out of the coma but seemed unable to speak and seemed to be very frightened. After some time he seemed to adjust and began to eat although without much appetite but he never said a word. Further, he began to gain back some physical strength, which was not evidently very great before his accident, and was able to move about.

There were no records on him, his clothing having been mostly burned, nor did anyone inquire for him and no one of his description showed up on the missing persons list. He couldn't speak and answered all inquiries with a shrug. They thought that he could understand some gestures, that he was not insane, and that putting him into a mental institution would not help him much. Since labor was very short they "farmed" him out and that is how he came to be working as a hand at Reid's spread (I'm beginning to talk like these people). During the three years he had been with Reid, he had gained strength but never entered into any conversation although he seemed to understand and usually to obey verbal orders. Reid had the impression that he was afraid of his voice and that he could speak if he wanted to.

I wanted to see again the site of the explosion, and especially wanted to see if I could detect any reason why the diamonds had melted. Because they were so busy we had not been able to get there this afternoon. I asked whether someone could take me there tomorrow, in which case I would stay another day. Reid said, yes, there was likely to be less work tomorrow and if I could put up with "Bo" he would have him take me there. This seemed to me to be a good chance to examine "Bo", to see if he knew anything about the 'burned' diamonds, and to have a general look around.

The next morning I went over to the Medical Center in Roswell and inquired about "Bo". An elderly doctor remembered him as an unusual case and went hunting through the records. He found that he had been admitted early morning of September 4, 1995 and had been listed as DOA. This had been reversed and after heroic efforts his life had been saved.

The story the doctor told was very much like that I had gotten from Reid. But **the date was striking.** This was the morning after the explosion at the Iverson ranch. Was it possible that "Bo" had been there and been blown some 10 miles west to land in a shallow pond? Clearly such an experience might make one silent forever, for if one told this tale, who would believe it?

Now it is pretty easy to see where this is heading. Since I knew what was on the Capitan Disk, I could easily speculate that "Bo" had come from outer space on the spacecraft that was to pick up the creature who wrote the disk (who passed on earth as Anton Mielke, at least part of the time). Evidently the spacecraft had exploded, possibly while still in the air, and had ejected "Bo" so that he traveled 10-12 miles and fortunately landed in a pond which ordeal he had survived. We had the possibility of a real authentic space creature right in our hands. But there were some difficulties. He could not, or would not, speak. He did not seem to understand much of what we said or asked him. He was very fright-ened of anything new. He would not, perhaps I should mention, ride in a car unless actually forced into it. Probably he had never been to any city, never ridden a train or plane, never seen television, although he must have heard radio. It was constantly on in the bunkhouse. He was sort of an indentured servant of a rancher who was a client if not employed by a firm, Iverson, that had dealings with the space world, at least in the person of Anton Mielke. Some employees of this firm also recognized and respected an archaic symbol, the winged disk. How were we going to get "Bo" to some place where we could learn from him, perhaps teach him how to talk, and find out about his origins? This was beyond me so I packed up and went back to Evanston and dumped it into Prof Aron's lap. Aron brought up even further difficulties, one of which was "how were we going to do this without letting the Iverson people know or guess what we were trying to do?" We mulled this over for two weeks, came up with several solutions, none of which would work, and finally settled on the following scenario.

We first thought that we could use some charity in Evanston and offer speech therapy, but we soon ran into mountains of red tape and we also did not want to identify where we were or why we were interested in "Bo". We finally settled on the idea that I would stop by Roswell about once a month and hope for some chance for us to contact "Bo". I therefore went to Roswell again and contacted the ranch manager, Reid. I took him to dinner this time at Carrizozo which had a surprisingly good restaurant. I indicated that I was in touch with a collector who was interested in unusual rocks and who had purchased one of his deformed diamonds. I told him that I came through Roswell about once a month and I would contact him to see if he had found any other unusual specimens. This I did and usually took Reid to dinner. I did not ask about "Bo" but in conversations about the ranch (after all there was little else to talk about) his name would come up and I gathered that the situation remained about the same. However, after about six months we got a break. Reid told me that "Bo" had contracted pneumonia and was recovering in the hospital. I hoped that it was the Eastern New Mexico Medical Center in Roswell and I went there the next morning. He had been transferred to a nursing home, a hospice called the New Dawn Rest Home on West 18th St. I went there immediately and learned that "Bo" was up and about, still weak, but the main problem was that he was disoriented. He kept wandering about and was in a state of dementia such that he could not be released on his own. I visited him and he seemed to remember me (it was some five months since I had seen him) but he was still as uncommunicative as ever. However, he seemed to be greatly interested in television. There were several sets blaring all the time (most residents were somewhat hard of hearing), not all tuned to the same station. I noted that he preferred landscape scenes rather than soap opera. The other noticeable behavior was that he listened and seemed to understand an old lady (Mrs. Josephine Silverstein) who chatted away merrily, but no one could understand her since she spoke in Yiddish mixed with a certain amount of Polish. I doubt whether it mattered since what she said was probably incoherent anyway. Yet "Bo" seemed to be rather alert to her babbling. I had thought that maybe a speech specialist could help him but after watching him in the "home", it occurred to me that maybe a trauma manager would help.

When I inquired, the nursing home referred me to the Physicians Bureau and after consulting them, they recommended a Dr. Jefferson Hughes whom I then contacted. He proved to be a rather short (about 5 ft. 5) bald little man with a pronounced British accent---possibly Oxford. He agreed to have a look at "Bo" and see what he could do. I gave him my phone number in Evanston, and left to return to civilization.

Two days later I got a call from Dr. Hughes saying that he had seen "Bo" and thought that he could do some good (of course, if I would pay for it). Hughes said that as a trauma expert he felt that "Bo" had suffered from "dissociative amnesia" but that he was recovering. He was still in a state which they would call "retrospective memory recollection" (How these boys love complex words). He also said that "Bo" was perfectly capable of making sounds other than "bo" which was his usually communication and from which his name originated. He said that "Bo" responded to his speech and that it was a pleasure to have someone listen and not frown at his English accent. I told him to continue. This went on, one or two sessions a week, until I returned to Roswell at the start of the next month. "Bo" was still at "New Dawn" but was improving and could possibly be released in a week or so. I went to see Dr. Hughes who said that "Bo" had spoken two words; "eiki" and "chawn" they sounded like and while they made no sense, "Bo" had seemed very pleased with them. When I called Prof. Aron that night, he was very excited. He said go back and see "Bo", wear your flying disk ring, and say "A-Gim Menzen" or "A-na Menzen" or "A-Na-Am Menzen". These are real sumerian words (you can find them in the Sumerian Dictionary, "Adapa" (Can be found at http://home.earthlink.net/index1. html#dict) but Aron said he really didn't know how to pronounce them and if I got no response, I should try different methods of saying these phrases. I asked him what they meant and he said that they meant "good to see you" or possibly "how are you" in ancient Sumarian. One could read the words but since the language had not been spoken for at least 3 millennia, no one knew how to pronounce them. So next morning I went to see "Bo" and tried them. At first, nothing. Then when I said "ANAM MEENZEEM" I got a smile and he said, plain as could be, but with an Oxford accent, "Cheerio, old boy". We'd made a breakthrough. Of all things, "Bo" could speak, and he could speak English.

I was shocked. I asked could he really speak English? He said yes, he could speak some. So I asked him why he did not speak earlier. He said, just imagine his situation. For the first year after his accident, he really could not remember a thing. Gradually the memory came back but he really could not understand what the men he was working with were saying until he got used to it. Even Mr. Reid, the ranch manager, was difficult to make out. So after living with them for almost a year, he should come out and speak English? What would they have thought? Could they have understood his type of English? Then, he would have to explain who he was and how he got there. The old story of being a nephew of a Brazilian diamond miner would not work, not after what had happened. So he just had to remain quiet until he could figure a way out. This nursing home seemed to offer some possibilities and Dr Hughes, the trauma expert, was most helpful—and besides he could understand most of what the doctor said when he was not being technical. He was almost ready to talk to him, making him think that he had brought him around when I had startled him with that old archaic greeting which they sometimes used, mostly in jest. What did I say, I asked. He said, you said "How be it with you". I asked what language was it, was it old Sumerian? Good lord, bloody no. He'd never heard of them, but the words were from a language that had disappeared centuries ago. I told him that we had found cuneiform tablets with this language at a place called Sumer and had become able to read them. We therefore called the language and the civilization that used it, the Sumerian civilization. This did not interest him much. But he said, now that you know, what do we do now? He clearly needed help to get out of his situation into the real world. I told him that I didn't know what we could do, but that he should feign confusion for a few more days and I hoped that Prof. Aron could come up with a plan. I promised to be back the next day.

I called Prof. Aron and we discussed, over the phone, what to do. We thought of several schemes, but none would really work so finally I was left with the order—"bring him to Evanston, even if you have to kidnap him". It seemed I had to kidnap him, sort of with or without his consent, but I thought that he would come willingly. But how to do this without attracting considerable unfavorable attention or having him hiding and on the run for the rest of his life. That was the real problem. Further, his life, until we could get him away, had to be perfectly normal, with no hint of his possible change of fortune. If only he could disappear quietly. But that, it seemed to me, was both the problem and the answer. Maybe he had wandered off and some wild animal had taken him. Was this likely enough so that search for him might soon decline? How to make him disappear?

I eventually concocted the following plan. "Bo" returned to the Iverson ranch, kept on with his work but tended to be a little erratic and would wander off, and seem to get lost every once in a while. There was forming in my mind the idea that on some dark night, he might wander off, get near a highway where I could pick him up. So I spent the rest of the day traveling these highways looking for small side roads going in the direction of the ranch, hoping to find a place where I could wait unnoticed and where he could find me. You expect me to say that indeed there was such a road, but in truth there was nothing suitable. The few roads led to houses (shacks mostly) occupied by ranchers or by ranch hands and there was nothing else.

So I had to devise another plan or two but when I went back to the New Dawn Home the next morning a further complication arose. "Bo" had been restless the night before, whether deliberately or because he now saw a way out of his dilemma. But the Home had now limited the visits to 10 minutes. Further the place was crowded and we could not risk people seeing us together speaking English. I quickly outlined my plan. It takes a little longer to write out than to speak but still it took longer than I liked. I didn't want to be identified as the guy who came to visit "Bo" before he disappeared. The next time I came I would have to alter my appearance. Wearing a mustache is a little too obvious and I couldn't grow bald overnight so I really had to settle on the plan in the few short minutes we had.

The plan was the following. One night (generally Saturday) when there were few people around the ranch, "Bo" would leave the sleeping bunkhouse at about 1 to 1:30 A.M. and walk south four miles until he reached Highway NM 48 where he would take cover in a ditch. I would drive in a clockwise direction from Capitan along 48 to 368 to the town of Hondo, then US 380 to Capitan and then around the circle again. This I would do starting at 3 A.M. and again at 4 A.M. If "Bo" saw me coming he would get on to the shoulder of the highway and wave his hat at me. To identify me I would carry a detachable spotlight operating on the car battery which would be focused on the center of the road. All of this I conveyed to him rapidly and set the first attempt at the Saturday, two weeks from now. If that did not work we would try again the week following on Sunday (which was also generally quiet since the boys were sleeping off their night on the town).

With that I left. I could not leave him a cellular phone or even a compass since they might be discovered. I hoped that he would be out of the Dawn House and that he would remember.

On the designated night I made circuit at the specified 3 A.M. Nothing. But on the second circuit, starting at 4 A.M. I saw a "body" in the ditch. It was "Bo". He had passed out, mostly because he was scared, I think. But at least I got him into the car, where he recovered. I got him to put on. the wig (and had to explain why) and we drove off just under the speed limit and ended up about noon at a small motel about 40 miles west of Wichita, Kansas. And late the following afternoon we got to Evanston. Prof. Aron greeted "Bo" warmly and. I think, would have gotten right down to the work of questioning him, if I had not intervened and pointed out that we had to let Bo get used to his new bunkhouse and to the elevated trains and bustle of near-by Chicago. We saw nothing in the papers about anyone disappearing from the Capitan ranch.

So Wednesday we rested and "Bo" got a little used to his new quarters. But on Thursday after a large breakfast, "Bo" and Aron went into Aron's study and had a conversation with "Bo". Aron first asked him what had happened that he was injured when he was first found. He said the bloody ship had blown up. Apparently they were going along nicely when they hit something just before they were to land and the next thing he knew was that he was in a hospital, that it was some weeks later, and he was not in good shape. He could not remember anything. He could not understand what the people were saying nor could he speak except to sort of grunt. As time went on he gradually found his memory returning, but he still could not speak properly. Aron asked what ship had blown up? Was he traveling in an airplane. Yes and no, "Bo" said. He was certainly traveling in the air but in an EASP airship (which he called a "Sham", a term Aron recognized as meaning "sky chamber" in ancient Sumerian). We asked what EASP was and he said that it was an Electronic Assisted Sound Power. Now we had seen this on the Capitan disk, but we still didn't know what it really was. Bo was rather at a loss to explain it since he said he was not an engineer, a physical scientist, or an astronomer. When asked what he was, he said that he was a nutritionist. I assumed that he would be interested in calories and good and bad cholesterol. But no, he was very much interested in what he had eaten at the ranch, in the hospital, and here in Evanston. He began to question us about the ingredients that went into these foods, how long they were cooked, etc. "Bo" said our foods all tasted rather peculiar to him—much too bland He liked more flavor. So he rather liked the Mexican food at the ranch. I had to conclude that he was not a nutritionist in our sense, but was a cook-presumably a gourmet cook. He said that he was trained as a "nihatim" which Aron said meant "cook" and that probably his English teacher translated this as 'nutritionist'. Much of the information I got from

279

"Bo" came almost causally when we were discussing something else. The situation was that Aron questioned him perhaps 6 hours a day. Most of this time I had other duties so I was not present. Prof. Aron will no doubt write a book or two about what he found out. But much of this I do not know. From Aron's point of view there are two things of interest. One was the nature of the language and how it had evolved from ancient Sumerian. The other was how the society had evolved over the centuries and the comparison between where we were and where they were, since the two cultures had evolved essentially independently. Or had we? There was always the question as to whether they had intervened in our development every 3,600 years or maybe every 60 years. I got little direct information. Much of what I can describe about his planet is interpreted from what he said or what I have deduced from the situation. Prof Aron was very busy with his projects and did not want to discuss this "extraneous" information with me.

They evidently had cities, and 8-10 story buildings, (such as were in downtown Evanston) but they seemed to have relatively little street traffic. "Bo" often remarked on how crowded the streets were. They did not seem to have the equivalent of automobiles, but seemed to have what we could call 'public' transportation but evidently more efficient than ours since everybody seems to use it. He also remarked about how noisy it was. Evidently these vehicles, through driven by electronically enhanced sound, were quieter. They did not seem to run on the ground but rather hovered over it and there were no tracks. Indeed when the first "L" went by Bo was greatly frightened and I had quite a time getting him to accompany me to the "Loop" on the "L". Going down to Chicago rather startled him and he was greatly impressed by the small size (and general shoddiness) of the houses and stores we could see from the "L". He was greatly impressed by the taller buildings and gazed in awe from the top of the Tribune Tower. I gathered that they had few buildings taller than 10 stores and that they were more massively built than ours. They did not have steel frame construction, being, I gathered, constructed from interlocked stone blocks or some kind of artificial stone (concrete?). They did, however, have large sheets of glass. I gather that they were much farther away from their star than we are from the Sun and that illumination was perhaps a tenth of what we get. As such, the plants tended to grow slowly and those he recognized as being similar to his (I took him to the botanical garden for this purpose), were mostly shade loving and seem to be largely ferns. They did have wheat and barley, mostly of the short stemmed variety. He was quite familiar with water plants and particularly remarked upon their similarity to "Lotus". I remembered that the Lotus was the symbol of life in ancient Egypt. Although what is commonly called Lotus here today differs from the Lotus described by ancient Egypt, we still do have the plant that the Egyptians called Lotus. And we know it is the same plant because it has a peculiar fatty acid and lipid composition which is identical to the lotus leaves used in wrapping mummies. It appears that the ancient Egyptian Lotus had a 'narcotic like' ingredient somewhat stronger than the present day 'ginseng'. The Egyptian Lotus was supposed to have medicinal and possibly hallucinogenic properties since it was widely used in religious ceremonies and almost all Egyptian temples have it as a decoration especially as the capital of their pillars.

I took Bo on rides on the elevated trains (the "L" as it is known in Chicago). We not only went from Evanston to the Loop, but also from the Loop to Oak Park in the west to the South Chicago sections to Lake Calumet. Incidentally the "Loop" is a square of elevated tracks in the center of Chicago. Trains from the north come down, go around the corners of the square and then head north again. Those from the south and west also go around the loop and head back to their origin. The loop is thus the major area of exchange. Today this is partially replaced by subway but the old "Loop" still exists and we always tried to take the elevated rather than the subway sections. From what we could see from the "L", "Bo" judged that their largest city (Ur) was not as large as Chicago, but fairly close. Since the area we looked at has about 8 million people I guessed that Ur held about 7 million. Bo said that there were five other major cities (named Harran, Akked, Kis, Elubad, Isin), and most were about half the size of Ur (each about 3.5 million) so the total urban population would, by this guess, be about 25 million. They did not have large farms as we do in the States, but rather small holdings surrounding the villages, much like the system of farming peasants in Europe. They needed the fertile land so badly that each village might consist of one 4-5 story building where all the population lived and surrounding land was all under cultivation. I gathered that the fertile land stretched perhaps 500 miles from the 'sea'. I find it difficult to estimate how many people live in the farming areas but Bo thought that less than a third of the people were engaged in farming, so that would bring the village population to no more than 10 million. Adding a few more that we may have forgotten to count, I would guess that the total population of the planet, presumably about the same size as ours, to be about 50 million. We have 6 billion (6000 million) so the population was rather sparse, limited. But it turned out from further conversation that the rest of the land, while not very fertile, and rather arid, but it did support an additional population called Akids (incidentally, the ancient Sumerians had neighbors called Akkadians) who were mostly nomads, lived in tents and cultivated animals resembling sheep and camels. The Akids were rather taller and thinner than the inhabitants of the fertile lands and had beards and long hair. They were regarded as somewhat primitive and uncivilized. I have often wondered why shaving was regarded as an index of civilization. The Roman legions were all clean-shaven (it was a test of the sharpness of the swords). Yet the ancient Sumerians, as shown on monuments and gateways have trimmed beards. "Bo" said that the beard, when fashioned and trimmed, was the prerogative of royalty, but that the Akids were an unkempt group and were too lazy to shave. He also said that over the years, possibly due the restricted diet (rather short on meat) most civilized people came to have very little facial hair and most males were bald. I would guess that there were perhaps 10 million Akids so the total population of the planet was around 60 million, roughly one hundredth of the population of the earth.

It seemed that there was a king (or emperor) called "Enil-Ki" (we had seen this on the Capitan Disk) and there were princes ("Nir-gal") for each of the major provinces (including that of the Royal city, Ur). In addition there was an "operation committee" (OC) which had three divisions: government (GOC), science and education (SOC), and living conditions (LOC). Each of these committees had about 30 members, rather well trained and experienced. The SOC (Scientific Operating Committee) which sponsored and controlled "Bo", was mostly scientists, mathematicians, astronomers, university presidents, etc.; a very erudite and intelligent group. However, "Bo" said that they had too much control. One could not undertake a study, (of pepper, for example, which "Bo" had wanted to do), without their approval, funding and that this meant long detailed "research plans", projected benefits etc.

Further the members were so prestigious that they did not like to consider anything really new, so that progress was slow. It was not clear to me how committee members were selected but there were the usual clans and cabals and certain groups seemed to be excluded and one of these excluded groups was "nutrition" to which "Bo" belonged. He was appointed to this earth mission because of his great intelligence and also because he had an uncle in some important position who could recommend him.

It seems that everybody, even the Akids, go to school until the age of about 20 years (earth years). Somewhat less than half do not go on. These become the laborers, carpenters, plumbers, even electricians. Then over half go to school for another 10 years and are trained for the professions. Some go on for another 10 years. Actually it does not seem to be too different than our system. These developmental stages seem to have more to do with physical development rather than the length of the year or the amount of sunlight. However, the lines between the workers, the professions, and the superior grades seem to be more rigid and while exceptional people with exceptional needed skills or knowledge can cross these lines, it is difficult and rare. Everyone is guaranteed living quarters, food, medical care and some entertainment. They have something resembling television, but I could get no further information on it. They seem to have amateur and professional games, something like football, basketball, etc. (at least "Bo" was not surprised to see these on our television). Gradually he got used to his wig and was not so frightened of new things, so Prof. Aron told me to take him out and get him familiar with everyday (if somewhat elevated) life. So we went to the movies, stage shows (Evanston has an excellent theater right on the border with Chicago), restaurants etc. He was especially interested in the latter, and kept urging me to try certain ones he read about in the newspapers. (When he first encountered a newspaper he was astounded, evidently they did not have them.) He tended toward Spanish and Mexican food and was especially interested in spices. He wanted to go into the kitchens, and after we had been in a restaurant a few times and were sort of regarded as old customers, we were given tours, or just allowed to go in and watch. "Bo" would talk to the cooks and ask them where they got various ingredients, and would then urge me to go buy them for him. He wanted to cook meals for us so we let him into our kitchen, and he prepared some excellent meals, although somewhat peppery for my taste.

We now ran into another problem. "Bo", in addition to becoming fat and refusing to take any exercise (this "physical" work being only for the "lower classes") became surly, uncooperative and bored. I was at a loss to figure out how to amuse him. Then it occurred to me, why should I amuse him? Let him find his own amusement. Maybe we should get him a job to keep him busy. Since he was so interested in cooking, why not get him a job in a restaurant? I watched the newspaper and finally found an ad for the Bangalore Restaurant in the Wilson Park area, reachable from Evanston by the "L" with only one change. They were looking for a cook.

This area had been largely taken over by immigrants from India and I thought that maybe some of them would like the food that "Bo" liked to make. So we went there and "Bo" applied, and since they were rather desperate for help, they took him on, at a little below the minimum wage. But "Bo" loved it. First he did routine things, but he got along well with the other workers, and especially the manager, so they soon let him try some of his own specialties (he brought down some of the spices we had purchased for him). After about a month he was made a cook, not just a cook's assistant. Now it was something of a hassle to ride the "L" each day especially since he worked from 11 A.M. to 9 P.M., so we found an apartment for him close to his work. He became much happier, and somewhat thinner since he was getting some exercise at his work. I suggested that he take some courses at the Culinary Institute on Chicago Avenue near the Northwestern University Downtown Campus. This he did (we paid for them) and he received his certificate. He is still at the Bangalore now as chief cook, but I hear that he is considering moving to the "Star of India" at the Drake Hotel downtown. At least, however, he has become integrated and a useful and successful member of society.

But what should we do with this information? It tended to confirm ancient legends, it gave us some index of life on another planet, indeed, it seemed to provide good evidence that there was life on other planet in the universe and that the living beings were much like us and that they were in some ways as intelligent as we (if that is a compliment). Should we make this public?

Now suppose that we alerted the Space Agency to expect a visit from "extra terrestrials" sometime between 2001 and 2015. We would get a hearing, I am sure, before we were confined to the nearest insane asylum. Suppose we showed this to people who believed that the earth had already been visited. The evidence we had was really no better than theirs, and if they talked to "Bo" (how could we prevent this?) his life would be ruined and this would be a tragedy since he was now doing what he loved to do. Other outlets were equally unpromising. We finally decided that I should write a "novelette" and get it published (if I could) and then when in 2011 or following, a space ship (or even the planet) was detected we could say "We told you so". In the meantime, Prof. Aron would continue his work on the language and the customs, civilization, organizations, etc. on the planet and eventually publish the 10 volumes that he had in mind. So this is what we did and this is why you are reading this today.